When *the* Game Changes

losing my mum and finding myself

EVANKA OSMAK

with KRISTINA RUTHERFORD

Published by Simon & Schuster

New York Amsterdam/Antwerp London
Toronto Sydney/Melbourne New Delhi

# SIMON & SCHUSTER CANADA

A Division of Simon & Schuster, LLC
166 King Street East, Suite 300
Toronto, Ontario M5A 1J3

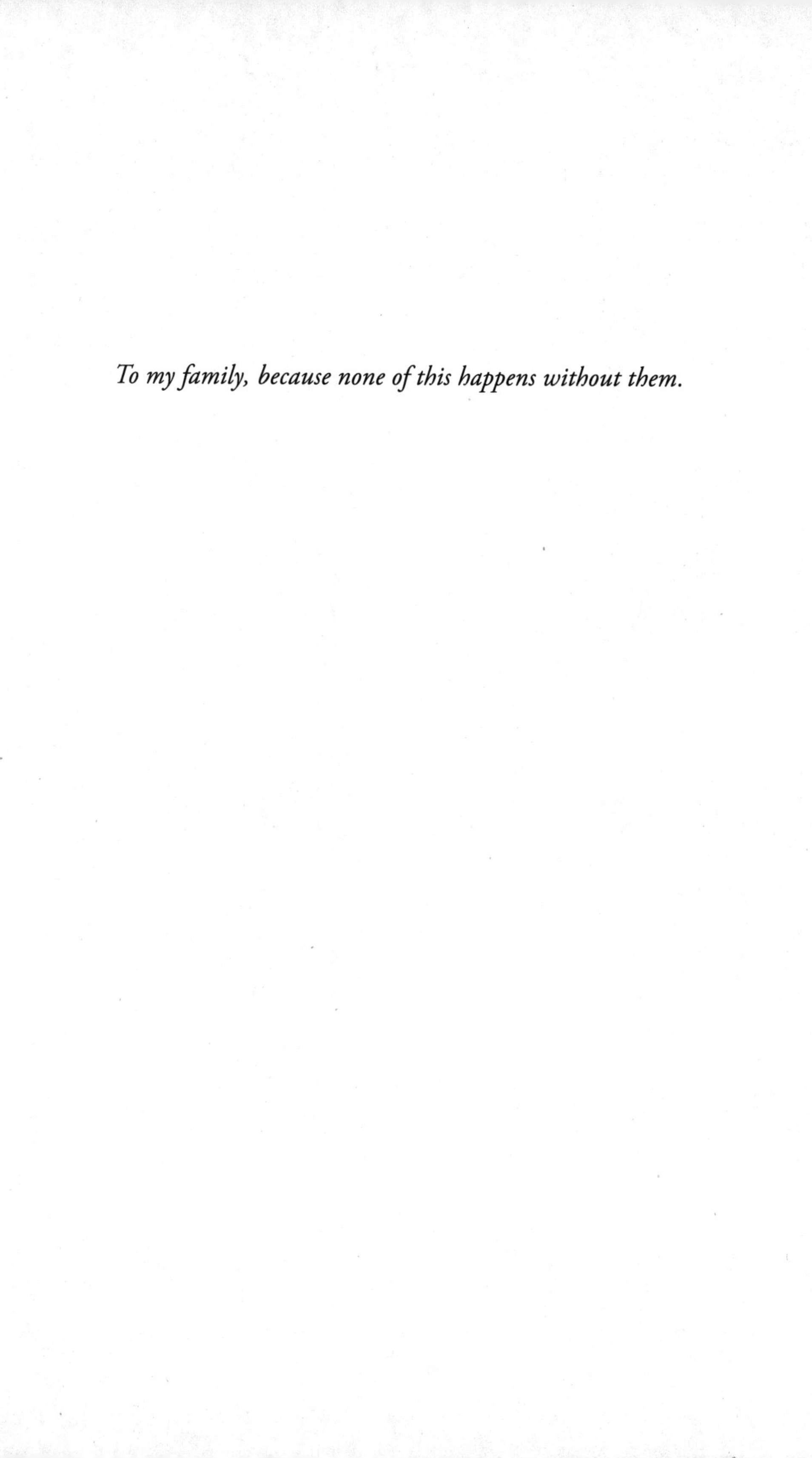

To my family, because none of this happens without them.

Contents

Forty-Year-Old Rookie

Nerves. Glee. Pride. Embarrassment. Fear. Exhilaration. What the heck am I doing here?

I keep looking down at my gloves. Am I holding my stick properly? Do I have a good enough grip on my helmet? Because if I drop it, the last thing I need is more attention on me during the national anthem. I feel like everyone already knows I don't belong.

I look to my right, and there's Hockey Hall of Famer Lanny McDonald. Wendel Clark's moustache catches my eye. I'm standing beside Olympic gold medallist Blayre Turnbull. How is she looking so casual? Though surely if anyone knows how to stand during the Canadian anthem, it's an Olympic gold medallist. Is her hair in a ponytail or did she leave it down? I should have put mine up.

Across the ice, I see more familiar faces. There's Darcy Tucker and Bobby Ryan. They know I'm nervous. They're chuckling and grinning at me—not in a mean way, but in an "I've never seen her like this before!" and a "This will be fun!" kind of way. But . . . will it be fun?

Darcy and Bobby played in the National Hockey League. I can't skate backward. I can stop . . . sort of, and only on one side. It's not an immediate stop. It's similar to when you're driving and you approach a yellow light and slow down with caution. Not ideal when the game moves back and forth at lightning speed.

More than three thousand fans are in the stands watching. It's January 20, 2023, and this is the Hockey Day in Canada alumni game in Owen Sound, Ontario, part of a weeklong celebration of the sport. Every Canadian team in the National Hockey League plays tomorrow, and all the action will air on the country's number one sports television network, Sportsnet. More than 8 million people will take in the broadcast.

I'm used to being part of that broadcast, with a microphone clipped to me and a video camera on me while I fill sports fans in on what's going on, or what's coming up. I'm an anchor for Sportsnet, and it's a job I love, one I've been doing for fifteen years. I help deliver the nightly sports news across the country, talk fans through highlights and lowlights. I interview athletes, coaches, general managers, and analysts. I tell fans what happened at sporting events.

I'm not used to being part of the sporting event, like I am today. And so I'm standing here, trying to look like a hockey player, and feeling like an absolute fraud. (That's also how I feel writing this book. I'm not an author, but here I am trying to get over feeling like an absolute impostor.)

I started playing hockey a couple of years ago, at the age of forty-one. My five-year-old son, George, is probably better than I am. Please don't tell him I said that.

What right do I have to be here with all these pros?

I glance down at my stick again. Why do I feel so awkward holding it when everyone else seems so natural, like that stick is an extension of their arm? Am I supposed to be looking somewhere other than at the players on the ice with me? Should I look up at the Canadian flag? Is it obvious that I'm not paying attention to the anthem?

I need to take some deep breaths. I'm trying to remind myself that this is just for fun. I won't get fired for falling or laughed at for trying. But I'm still uncomfortable being so far out of my comfort zone.

And then, silence. The singer stops singing. The crowd claps and cheers. All the players across from me and beside me have dispersed.

So here we go. Game on?

Three shifts in, my linemate Wendel Clark threads me a pass. The Toronto Maple Leafs legend is determined to set me up for a goal, and he told me to stand in front of the net with my stick on the ice. He told me to be ready to snipe (that's what we call scoring).

Clark fires the puck my way. I have a clear shot at the net if I can get a handle on it. My mind is racing as I get ready for the pass.

Don't screw this up!

Should I try a one-timer? (No. Never.)

What if I fall while I'm shooting?

And seriously, the biggest question of all: *How in the world did I get here?*

Fresh Ice

I do a lot of "Where were you when" moments for my work when I'm talking about big sporting events in history, so maybe it's no coincidence that my book starts with one of those as well.

Where were you in 2021? Or rather, *how* were you in 2021?

I remember it all too well.

It's May of 2021, and I'm not doing great. The world is not in a good place. None of us are thriving. We're in the middle of a pandemic, and the COVID-19 virus has changed everything about the way we live and interact and work. Even the way we think.

There is good news, though. Thankfully, things are improving. It seems we're through the worst of COVID (we truly hope). I'm feeling much less isolated than I was a few months ago. It has been ages since I've seen my girlfriends, but we've started to interact as the world opens up and it's been safe to hang out. We had drinks the other night at Betsy's house, and laughed behind our masks. It felt amazing. Instead of running outside by myself or lifting weights alone in my living room to get the exercise I need to feel good, now I do masked-up boxing classes with my friends. Things are much better than they were.

Another reason the sense of isolation has lifted for me is because I'm coming off a yearlong maternity leave, and I'm back to work. Our one-year-old, Blake, and our four-year-old, George, are now being taken care of during the day by a nanny, and we're so thankful to have that support. It's key for my husband, Adam, and me, because he works long hours running his own business and I work nontraditional hours at Sportsnet. I head to the studios in downtown Toronto around six p.m. and I don't get home until about two or three the next morning.

I'm so excited to be back at work. It gives me the jolt of energy I've needed. My job is challenging, it's fun, and I love my co-workers, including my co-anchor, Ken Reid, even if the guy is the biggest pain in my ass and makes fun of me like no other. Nobody throws me under the bus like Ken. He's still somehow one of my best friends. (Ken, that's the nicest thing I'll say about you in these pages.) I'm coming up on fifteen years at Sportsnet, and I feel lucky. This is a dream job, and I didn't get here on a typical path, which makes me feel even more fortunate.

But I also can't help but feel disconnected going back to work, and I know a lot of us do. Many of my colleagues don't go into the office anymore if they're not absolutely needed on-site. There used to be eight people in our control room. Now there's a skeleton crew of four. I'm doing my own hair and makeup, which is unusual (this is not a strength, and how the heck do you put on fake eyelashes? No amount of YouTube videos can help me. I give up!). Ken, who now expertly (he thinks) dabs his face with powder on a nightly basis, sits six feet away from me on the desk. We used to be nearly elbow to elbow, close enough for a high five. But so much about work has changed. So much of the social interaction I'm used to at the office is gone.

And so I feel a bit like a hamster on a wheel. I wake up every day and think about how today looks so much like yesterday. The variables: who's taking care of the kids, who's getting groceries, who's cleaning the house, who's making dinner . . . blah blah blah. I work, sleep, wake up, and do it all over again. This is Adam's routine, too. We have a schedule. And it's easy to keep doing the same things every day, and harder to work in a disruption that'll throw things off.

But I really need to throw things off.

Because honestly, I can't help but wonder: *Is this it? Is this all there is?* And *is it going to continue like this forever?* I'm forty-one years old and this is kind of boring. *I'm* kind of boring. I'm too young and too curious to be so set in a routine. I'm managing all these adult things, making sure my kids are having fun and learning and meeting new friends, but I'm forgetting about fun and play and challenges for myself.

I can't remember the last time I felt uncomfortable or scared while I was learning a new skill. I don't have hobbies. When was the last time I really challenged myself, or made a new friend? I have the best girlfriends, but we don't see each other enough, and when we do, we're going for wine or coffee. No, I don't want to just read some book and sit around and talk about it, either. That's not enough. I really want to *do* something!

Adam and his friends do something every Thursday night—they play hockey. It's the same ritual every week. Since I'm at work, we have to get a babysitter while he's on the ice. But we know that playing hockey with his buddies is an outlet for him. After a tiring day or long week, it's one thing he always looks forward to.

He jumped into the sport when most Canadians do: as a kid. It was never about making it as a pro—that reality gets dashed quickly when you see the competition. (Though my dreams of making it as a pro are still very much alive. Ha!) When I ask Adam what it is about hockey that keeps him returning every week for the past thirty years, his answer is quick: "It's pure fun."

And look, I remember the pure fun that sports provide. I've loved sports my whole life. But I'm embarrassed and shocked to say that it has been more than a decade since I last played a team sport. That was Ultimate Frisbee, after university.

The last time I set foot in a locker room and put on gear while I chatted with teammates was my last year of high school field hockey. In 1997.

When I think back to my greatest memories from high school, many of them are being in that dressing room, being on that field, playing and working together with a team. That sense of accomplishment you feel with other women, working toward a common goal together—I can't think of anything more powerful.

Why hadn't I done that in nearly *twenty-five years*?

And so there I was in September of 2021, taking George to play in his first hockey game. He was sitting in the locker room with kids who were teammates and would soon become friends. He was out on the ice learning skills. He was falling. Laughing. *Playing*.

And it hit me: I should do that.

A friend had told me about this hockey league called Sister Sports, near where I live in the north end of Toronto. Right after George's skate, I looked up the league, which is for women of all skill levels. Players who have been lacing up for decades and rookies who just switched to hockey skates, like me. The first skate of the season was . . . two days away.

I don't have time to think about it. To question my decision. To remind myself I've never played hockey or worn hockey skates or, or, or . . .

I find the league's sign-up link, where there are three levels on offer. Level one, if you have some experience. Nope. Level two, if you have a wee bit of experience. Nope. Level three, the lowest, if you're an absolute beginner who wants to be part of skills sessions, and not just jump right into games. Yep, that's me. *Click.*

I'm really doing this. But the first skate is less than forty-eight hours away, and I need . . . a full set of equipment. I really need to spring into action here.

The next morning, I walk into Just Hockey Source for Sports. Connor McDavid's face is everywhere. Sidney Crosby's on a few posters, too. There's a full wall of skates. A wall of sticks. So much hockey tape. The place is pretty empty, which makes sense because it's a weekday. Thank goodness there aren't a lot of people here, so I won't have to fight for anyone's attention. I need a dedicated salesperson.

But I'm as ready as I can be. I'm holding a pen and a handy list of all the gear I'll need, which I found on the Sister Sports website. I plan to check off every item I get to make sure I don't miss anything. And let's face it, I'm a salesperson's dream. I need *everything*. You could definitely sell me on stuff I don't need, since I wouldn't know the difference. Can you show me your best helmet? That's the one for me. Also, where are the jills? Adam told me a jill is basically a jock for women. I've never played a sport where my lady parts need protection. My teeth, yeah . . . my shins, sure. But this crotch protector is a first. I can tell hockey's gonna be tough.

The sales guy who helps me is so sweet, and clearly I'm not his usual customer. Oddly, he doesn't have a ton of experience outfitting a tall, forty-something woman for her rookie season. I'm five foot ten, with broad shoulders and size 11 feet. He's finding the sizing . . . difficult.

"You're a large, but you're not a large!" he tells me, sweating nervously, holding up a T-shirt-style neck guard, which looks oversized, but seems like it'll make my wardrobe choices easier. Perfect.

I'm trying to keep from laughing while he frets over calling me "large."

"My wife would kill me if she heard me say that!" he says.

"It's okay!" I tell him. "I'm fine being a large!"

This Just Hockey store has some gear made specifically for women, but there's nothing in my size. Most of the equipment is made for men. I'm used to that, I guess—my running shoes are men's.

I'd never really given it much thought, but it hits me as I'm trying on shoulder pads that make me feel like I'm wearing my dad's gear: When I play hockey, I'm going to be wearing something that's definitely not made for me. It's made for a man. I have to compromise.

And when I actually think about it, it's not cool. I have boobs. I have curves. I don't have a man's body and I shouldn't have to jeopardize my comfort.

I decide I'll shoot right because I golf right. That sounds right . . . right? But how do I pick out the curve on my stick? This stick says "McDavid" down the side. Connor McDavid scores lots of goals in the NHL, and he's a no-brainer future Hall of Famer. That's the stick for me. I plan on being a real sniper. Ha!

I buy a bag without wheels, because George carries his bag, so I'll carry mine, too. I have to woman up.

I am seriously invested now.

When I walk into North Toronto Memorial Arena for my first skate the very next morning with that new bag slung around my shoulders, I'm sweating. That's probably nervous energy. But I feel good knowing that most of the women hitting the ice today are beginners like me. We're in the same boat.

I get to the dressing room and sit down in an open space between two women. I smile awkwardly, though nobody can see my mouth, since we're all wearing masks because of COVID. They come off once we put our helmets on and head out to the ice.

Even though I can't see people's faces, it's immediately crystal clear as I look around that I'm the only true rookie here. I'm the only newcomer. The other women are all chatting, and they know each other's names. Their equipment doesn't look new. It smells a bit like Adam's. (That's not a compliment.) They're talking about another league they've played in together. My eyes widen as I listen to them talk. I breathe heavily into my mask.

"Cheryl, glad to see you back for another season!"

"Mandy, how's your knee doing? All better?"

"Irene, did you play summer hockey this year?"

These women are already hockey players.

I am the only person in the room with zero hockey experience. Some of these women have played a couple of years, and some even played as kids.

I am in my own boat. And I am so, so intimidated by this group.

What was I thinking?

I do the only thing I can think of. I wait for a break in the conversation and say: "Hi, I'm Evanka. I've never played before. Ever."

A couple of women say, "Hi" in return, and "Welcome," and

that's the end of our chat. Okeydoke. There's no coddling, no special tips or wisdom for the awkward tall lady who's playing for the first time today. We've all signed up for hockey, and this is it.

I tell myself I'll be okay, and I lean down and open my bag. Everything smells new. I even left the price tag hanging off my shin pads. I rip it off. Tell me you're brand-new without telling me you're brand-new, right? *Oof.*

Okay, all my gear is here. Now how in the heck do I put it on?

Nobody has ever sat down with me and told me where to start. I'm trying to remember how I helped George get ready for his first skate a couple of days ago, and what went on first. I'm also scanning the room to make sure I'm doing what the other players are doing. But I don't want to be the new girl that stares.

I start getting dressed as best I can. I put my jill on first, because that makes sense. Shin pads. Socks. I tie up my skates. Crap! I forgot my pants. I have to pull those on over my skates, and that's a tight squeeze. Luckily, I don't rip the pants. Here's hoping nobody saw that struggle.

I wiggle my toes in my skates. I think I did a pretty good job tying them—I've tied George's up plenty of times. And wow, do mine ever feel good on my feet. It's already so different from my past experiences with skates.

As kids, my older brother, Nicholas—Nick—got hockey skates and my older sister, Katrusha—Kay—and I had figure skates. It was so painful for me in those narrow white skates with the toe pick. My foot felt squeezed, and there wasn't any ankle support. I hated skating as a kid. I didn't want to be cold and uncomfortable.

Putting my size 11 feet in hockey skates is like a revelation. Skates are actually comfortable. My ankles are supported.

And gosh, do I ever need any support I can get.

I put on my helmet. Then I realize I forgot my jersey.

Adam had thrown one of his white jerseys in my bag the night before, but the woman sitting beside me sees me pull it out. "We're supposed to wear black," she tells me. Shoot. Why didn't I notice that in the email from the league? "Anyone have an extra black jersey?" I ask. Thankfully a woman on the other side of the room does and throws it in my direction.

She has extra jerseys in her bag. Does that mean she's really good?

The jersey she lent me is blank on the back. Nice. Maybe it's best I'm numberless so I can't get called out by the skills coach!

I'm sitting here feeling pretty good, now that I'm basically dressed, and with the proper jersey in hand. Little do I know the worst part is ahead: I have to get that jersey on.

I put my right arm through the sleeve, and as I'm pulling it over my head to put my left arm through, the Velcro is ripping off my elbow and shoulder pads. *Riiiiiiip.* The jersey is stuck on my massive shoulder pads. My arms are in the air above my head. I hear more Velcro tearing as I yank my numberless jersey down, and then pull it up to manoeuvre it over the back of my shoulder pads. I'm twisting. Yanking. Shifting.

Finally, I pull up on the jersey so it can have some hope of clearing my shoulder pads, and then I yank it down with a good amount of force. Whew. It's officially on.

I pull up the bottom of the jersey so I can re-stick all the Velcro that came undone on my elbow and shoulder pads. I make a mental note to search "How to put on your hockey jersey" on YouTube later.

I'm really sweating now.

I put the helmet on my head. The pressure I'm applying to my head to get the snaps on feels like overkill, but it's the only way. I know this much from getting George dressed.

I'm ready. A little tired. And very scared.

It's time to play hockey.

I stand up and grab my stick, the longest one in the room; it leans near the door with that McDavid curve. I amble down the hallway toward the ice, looking at the rubber floor, feeling like an overstuffed robot. I've never stood on blades wearing so much equipment before. But I'm so happy to be protected. I'll need it. My shin pads are hitting each other as I walk. *Clunk. Clunk. Clunk.*

That's when I see Coach Ethan. He's wearing a whistle around his neck and a big smile, and a Sister Sports hat and tracksuit. His eyebrows shoot up when he notices my twig (I already know that's what we call a hockey stick).

"That's way too long!" he tells me. "Chop a foot off the top when you get home. And make sure you throw on some tape."

Adam had cut my stick the night before, and it turns out he forgot tape and overestimated my height. *Thanks, honey.*

I look out on the ice, and a few women are already there. One is zipping around. Another looks a little shaky, but she can turn both ways and stop. It's clear I can't skate nearly as well as anyone here.

What have I gotten myself into? On a sheet of ice like this, I won't go undetected. I'm about to make a fool of myself.

Here goes nothing.

I step onto the ice and smack my stick down for support. Phew. I navigated that well! Good start. I take my first-ever stride in hockey skates, wearing all my brand-new equipment. I'm kind of skating. Success!

I look down at my shin pads again, which feel giant, and then . . . boom! I'm on my butt and my stick is flying through the air. *Crash!* It's embarrassing, but I'm definitely laughing on the inside. Self-deprecation is my thing.

A more experienced player—that's every other woman here—glides over, picks up my stick, and extends a hand to help me up. I mutter, "It's my first time playing hockey," and she pulls me up, hands me my stick, and then nods and skates off.

I start to glide again, shaky and slow, staring down at my feet and the ice beneath me. I keep skating, gaining momentum, but not too much. *Let's not get carried away, Osmak.* I'm looking around, making sure I hold my stick with just one hand like the other women are as they skate laps. As they lap me.

I'm extra careful as I go around the nets, because I don't want to fall into those iron posts, you know? That would really hurt. As I skate, I'm thinking about that, and about everything I still have to learn about this game.

And from this moment, I realize—no, I know, beyond any doubt—that I am absolutely hooked.

This Tuesday morning in September of 2021 is the start of my hockey career.

And what I don't know at this point is that my decision to play—to find camaraderie among women, to be on a team again and rediscover the joy and community that sport provides—is something I'll need more than ever. Because I am about to suffer the biggest loss of my life.

Soft and Strong

Throughout my life, my biggest influence, my guiding light—in my family, my work, my friendships—has been my mother, Jeannie. And I can't help but think that she helped shape my decision to take up hockey in my forties more than either of us realized.

I was about thirteen years old when I discovered that my mum had made an incredible decision when she was just a teenager herself. I'd always known that she had moved away from home at sixteen, but it wasn't until I was a bit older that I realized how brave she was to pick up and travel across the country on her own.

Mum grew up in the tiny town of Gilbert Plains, Manitoba, a farming community home to fewer than a thousand people, about a four-hour drive northwest of Winnipeg. She and her younger brother helped my grandparents out, but Jeannie didn't care for farmwork. Or animals. You can imagine how she felt about chores growing up.

"Farm life just wasn't for me," she'd tell Kay and Nick and me anytime we asked about her childhood. "As soon as I could, I knew I had to leave so I could see what else was out there."

So Jeannie left. Her family didn't have much money, but the moment my mum graduated high school, she hightailed it out of little Gilbert Plains with a plan in mind: to move to the (comparatively) booming metropolis of Windsor, Ontario, home to more than two hundred times as many people as where she was from, so that she could attend the University of Windsor. That was basically Jeannie's only option for a post-secondary education, because she could save money by living with her aunt and uncle, who had a home there.

Jeannie was the first person from her immediate family to attend university. It was a huge deal. She carved her own path, and back in the 1960s, when it would've been tough to do. Not only that, but at the University of Windsor, my mum studied physics and math, two disciplines that were dominated by men in those days. I wish I would've talked to her more about that experience, but I think that knowing she had done that herself emboldened me to make some of the decisions I did about my own schooling and career.

It was at university in Windsor that Jeannie met my dad and truly started to build the next chapter of her life. But the part that stands out to me most when I think about my sixteen-year-old mum with that fire in her belly, packing her bags and moving to a big city in Ontario, is that she was a self-starter, motivated to seek what she wanted in life.

As I learned later, my mum was the type of person who got shit done, and that was one of the earliest signs.

Jeannie rarely gave us kids advice about how to live our lives unless we asked her for it. She never sat Kay and Nick and me down and told us: "Be strong." Or "Don't care about what other people say." Or "Pursue your dreams." But she showed us all of that by the way she lived, and I now know that was intentional. I think for my siblings and me, knowing from an early age that our mum had picked up and moved to seek out the life she wanted for herself, it was just implied that we, too, would all go after what we wanted. It was assumed that we should all pursue what would make us happy.

After Jeannie had Kay, she decided to stay home. And so Kay and Nick and I were raised by a stay-at-home mom who also had a degree in science, physics, and math. Though we grew up in a household where my parents filled what you'd call traditional roles—my dad, Borden, worked long hours for a bank, while my mum stayed home to raise us—I wasn't brought up thinking girls stayed home and boys earned money. No way. And there are lots of reasons for that. Jeannie wasn't sitting around in an apron, sewing and cooking and doing laundry all day. She had such a vivid life outside of that. She'd go for walks with friends. She was in book clubs. She played golf. She gardened. She played tennis. She mah-jongged.

And she was so, so smart. Mum was the parent we would go to with homework questions. Not just because she was often the only one home at night, but because she was a whiz. The Master of Math and the Queen of Grammar.

Both Jeannie and Borden raised us kids equally, so chromosomes didn't determine a thing in our house. There were no traditional pink and blue roles. I'd take out the garbage. Nick would wash the dishes. Kay would cut the lawn. We were all treated the same.

Borden was the rule-maker, and he was strict about chores—we had to get those done on weekends. There were no sleep-ins, no lounging around watching TV. It was up and at 'em, get your chores done. And while you didn't want to get in trouble with my dad, you didn't want to get in trouble with my mum, either. She could be fierce and intimidating if we stepped out of line. Jeannie would ground us if it was warranted. Her wrath could be harsher than anything my dad would do.

Mum was the heart and soul of our family—with an edge. Her personality was both soft and strong. She was by no means a bulldozer or a CEO, but we all knew in my family that while Dad made the money, Mum was just as powerful in her role. She took care of bills, planned travel, signed us up for and carted us around to activities, helped us with homework, and made and planned meals. She was such a good cook, too: Her chicken was always perfect, her ribs fell off the bone, and meals were always healthy and served just as we were getting hungry, only after we'd all washed our hands.

She was the social butterfly, too, who could talk to anyone about anything and be the life of the party. We'd see that when neighbours would swing by to say hello and it would turn into an event. Mum would somehow have a bunch of food ready to go, matching place mats and napkins, drinks poured, music playing (sometimes her favourite, Rita MacNeil), and popcorn made for a movie night for the kids in the basement while the parents chatted and relaxed and drank wine upstairs. So often, we kids saw my mum having fun with friends. Even with the movie on at full volume in the basement, we could hear her laughing upstairs.

I'll never forget what Mum told me shortly after I had George in March of 2017, and what she reminded me after I had Blake three years after that. She said: "Don't forget about you, just because you're a mom. That's not all you are! Your life is not just about kids. What are you doing for yourself to make sure you're happy and engaged and thriving?"

Mum didn't dole out much life advice, but when she did, it was memorable.

When I had George and Blake, Jeannie didn't expect me to stay home while they were young and give up my career at Sportsnet for any amount of time, even though she'd been a stay-at-home mom herself. She wasn't critical when I went back to work six months after I had George. That's considered pretty quick in Canada, where a yearlong maternity leave is standard. When I went back earlier than that, Jeannie was supportive. "I know how much work means to you," she said. And she knew I worked in a competitive industry where it's easy to be forgotten or left behind. Most of all, she knew that I would be a better mother if I felt fulfilled professionally.

As a mom herself, Jeannie worked at pursuing her passions outside of her family so she could feel fulfilled and challenged. I grew up seeing that. I wanted to be like my mum in that way. And in a lot of other ways, too. I was really hoping I'd inherited her get-up-and-go attitude and her infectious energy.

Taking up hockey in my forties seemed to me to be one way I could live up to what my mum first told me after I had George, about making sure I have my own life and hobbies, outside family life. And in just telling my friends about my hockey journey, it's a message I've been spreading. Since I started playing, a few of my friends also decided they would take up a new activity themselves, or get back into one they stopped because other aspects of their life got in the way. My friend Steph played soccer growing up, but stopped in her twenties and then joined a new team at forty-one. My friend Christine had always wanted to paint, but never got started because life's routines kept humming along.

Best of all was my girlfriend Betsy, who had been taking hip-hop classes for exercise and for fun. But while she was watching her daughters perform, Betsy realized that she had never taken the stage in front of an audience herself, at least as an adult dancer. When she heard about me playing hockey, Betsy decided she would perform . . . for the first time in nearly thirty years.

I got to see Betsy's return to the stage firsthand one Sunday night in November of 2022. I clapped along. I smiled so hard. And when it was all over, I actually cried. I was so happy for my friend.

I'm playing hockey, Steph's playing soccer, Christine's painting, Betsy's dancing. It has all reminded me how important it is to find something, whether it's sports or art or another endeavour, to disrupt our everyday routines. How important it is to find and maintain our identities—especially as women—to have an outlet, to get our pulses racing as we learn something new or try out a new hobby or revisit an old one.

That's something Mum taught me years ago. As she'd put it: "Don't lose yourself."

How It Started

It was an absolute circus in downtown Toronto—the best kind. I'd never seen anything like it. Fans spilling over from the sidewalks into the streets, wearing blue and white jerseys, waving blue and white flags. Chanting, "Let's go Blue Jays!" Jumping. Dancing. It was euphoria. Mayhem. And I loved it.

I was thirteen years old, and piled into the family station wagon with my mum and my *tato*, which means "dad" in Ukrainian. We could barely drive through the streets because the crowd was swarming our car, and every other car there. Somebody actually even high-fived our station wagon. Somewhere out there my nineteen-year-old sister, Kay, and sixteen-year-old brother, Nick, were on foot. I stayed in the car with my parents, as per their request, probably because I'd just become a teenager. That was fine by me because I felt safer.

My dad was behind the wheel, wide-eyed, smiling, foot on the brake. We'd all just about lost our voices, but were using whatever we had left to cheer along with the crowd in the streets. Jeannie and Borden aren't even really sports fans, but they were swept up by the energy. My mum loves a good party, and what a great excuse for one. Queen's "We Are the Champions" was blaring from a nearby car. The horns were blasting from every car. Nobody was in a rush to get home. Heck, my dad turned *into* the crowded streets instead of beelining for the highway to get back to Oakville, where we lived. He wanted to be a part of the celebration, too.

We'd just come from the SkyDome, where we witnessed history. We saw Joe Carter round the bases, jumping and yelling with his arms up as he ran, and we jumped and yelled right along with him. His three-run home run had clinched the series. The Toronto Blue Jays were World Series champions, and for the second straight year. What a moment.

When Carter hit that home run, my whole family and I, along with everyone else in the stadium, went absolutely berserk. High-fiving each other. Throwing popcorn. And the noise was deafening. Cheering, screaming, and absolute joy were bottled up in the closed Dome—all exploding at the same moment. We were champions—again!

I was swept up in the excitement. Captivated. And I wanted that feeling all the time. I assumed the Jays would keep on winning because isn't that what happens? There I was, a teenager, present for one of the biggest moments in Canadian sports history, and naively thinking we'd have many more moments just like it.

My friend Lara and I made sure we relived the moment. The number of times we watched VHS tapes of the 1992 and 1993 World Series, pretending like we didn't know the outcome? Countless. We would watch game by game on the edge of our seats and then jump up and down, screaming, when they won.

My family was lucky enough to see that series-clinching 1993 World Series win in person because Tato got tickets through his connections at the bank. He never passed up on the chance to take us kids, and we never passed up on the opportunity to go. Jeannie always made sure it fit into our schedules, too—and how she managed that, I truly don't know. Three kids meant a lot of moving parts, but Mum always kept us going in the right direction, and on time. Jeannie wasn't big into sports—she and my dad curled when I was much younger, and that's about it—but she was into making sure we all enjoyed ourselves as a family, and she knew we would revel in the chance to be at a big game like this one. Kay, Nick, and I always recognized how special it was to get to see big sports moments live. It was a big deal every time.

People talk about "catching the sports bug," but I never really felt like I caught a bug. I just always loved playing and watching sports. I thought everyone else did, too. Seriously, who wouldn't enjoy sports? It felt natural to me.

I couldn't think of anything better than heading to a game and enjoying the sights and sounds in the amazing atmosphere of the stadium. Oh, and the food. Popcorn and hot dogs. Extra butter and ketchup for me, please. It meant driving or training in from Oakville to the big city, about a thirty-minute trip back then. It meant getting dressed up, leaving the house, and being entertained.

We went to the MLB All-Star Game in 1991. Many Toronto Blue Jays games. We saw the Toronto Maple Leafs again and again. And sometimes, it was just us kids: Kay and Nick and I were at Game Seven of the 1993 Eastern Conference Final when the Leafs lost to Wayne Gretzky and the LA Kings, an absolute heartbreaker. I'd never seen a crowd as deflated as the one that night at Maple Leaf Gardens. Some fans were in tears. All I remember hearing on the way out the arena doors that cold night was "How about them Jays?" And as a twelve-year-old, I thought it was kind of funny that they were so ready to move on from the season. (I guess Leafs fans have gotten used to moving on?)

But those are the moments that stood out to me most as a kid—not what happened on the ice or the field, but what was happening off it, and around it. Absolute euphoria in the case of the Blue Jays, and despair when it came to the Leafs that same year. That was what got me hooked on sports: not just the athletes, but the atmosphere around the games, the way people cared so much about wins and losses. I was happy to be there to take it all in. To cheer. To eat. To see the best in the world play. It was only as I got older that I realized a lot of my girlfriends didn't have the same interest in sporting events as I did. *How odd*, I thought.

Many of my most vivid childhood memories involved big games. And that's probably why my love of sports came so naturally, why I can't remember or picture my life without sports. It's such a big part of who I am. And it always has been.

In fact, I changed schools in grade six because I wanted to play sports. I was going to an all-girls school in Oakville; Kay, Nick, and I all went to private schools, and the ones on offer were gender segregated. My parents believed in sending all three of us to private school, in part because neither of them had ever had access to an education like that. There wasn't a private school in the tiny Manitoba town where my mum is from, and even if there was, her family couldn't have afforded to send her. So Tato and Jeannie agreed that a private school education was what they wanted for their kids. Back then, there weren't a lot of co-ed private schools in our town, especially beyond grade eight. So it was the all-girls school for my sister and me, while my brother started at an all-boys school called Appleby College on the west end of town.

I was always so envious of Nick because his school had so many sports fields and so many sports to play. At my school, St. Mildred's, outside of gym class there weren't any school sports, and it was a small campus with just one field out back. What I saw at Appleby was an opportunity to play every sport. I so badly wanted that for myself.

And then opportunity knocked when I was in grade five. I'll never forget when Mum told me: "Appleby College is opening up to girls." I begged my parents to apply, and we did. I got in, and I would be starting there in grade six, the youngest age Appleby accepted girls. My timing was perfect. I was over the moon!

Mum kept telling me how brave it was of me to be one of the first girls at the school. "It's a brand-new experience, and I'm so happy that you're going for it," she said.

But I didn't think of the move as brave at the time. It's true that I didn't have many close friends from St. Mildred's who were switching to Appleby, but I didn't care. That didn't faze me. I knew this is what I wanted to do, so my only feeling was excitement. Just think of all the sports I'd get to play and the fields I could run around on! It hadn't occurred to me then that just because they'd admitted girls into the school, didn't mean they'd create girls' sports teams. I just assumed there would be so many girls like me thinking the exact same thing, and that we'd all be teammates. It would be perfect. Appleby had tennis courts. Soccer fields. Football fields. A hockey rink (I didn't go in there, but looking back, I should have). A swimming pool. Beautiful trees, and a campus right on the water. The possibilities were endless.

But in the end, grade six had fifty or sixty boys enrolled, and only twelve girls. And since there were so few of us, the school wasn't exactly offering sports opportunities for us, since we could barely field a team. That meant if I wanted to be on a team, it had to be with the boys. I was taller than a lot of the boys, and I was pretty strong. To me, that just meant I'd be a good addition to the team.

I'll never forget the day of my soccer tryout. It was early fall, but it was hot. And I sweat a lot. It's not the greatest look when you're trying to act cool. I was sweating buckets on that beautiful Appleby grass, feeling lucky that I'd have a chance to play soccer for my school. I had figured there'd be a bunch of girls just like me who wanted to play on the team. But as the coach blew the whistle and we all gathered around, I saw about twenty boys . . . and one other girl. She was tall like me, with brown hair and beautiful blue eyes. When we noticed each other, we both smiled. We were in this together.

That blue-eyed girl with the brown hair was Lara. That was the very first time we met—and she's still one of my best friends today.

At the tryout, Lara and I ran beside each other during warm-up laps. We passed the ball to each other. We instantly clicked. And . . . we both made the team! Okay, I think everyone made it, if I remember correctly. But so what? Lara and I acknowledged early on just how cool this was: Here we were at a school that previously banned girls, playing on the boys' soccer team. And if there was any jealousy or resentment from the boys about us being there, we didn't feel it. We felt proud.

I remember Jeannie being so proud of me, too. She came to watch our team play. She brought orange slices. She cheered me on, and despite having two other kids to worry about, she tried to make all my games. I'm pretty sure she made every single one.

That's my mum for you: loving, supportive, and always there when you need her. Jeannie was the one you'd go to if you needed a hug or wanted to ask if you could sleep over at your friend's house that night, or to see if you could get out of going to church on Sunday to do something fun instead. Like watch the VHS tape of the 1993 World Series with Lara.

Jeannie wasn't what you'd call an athlete, but she was the one who signed Kay, Nick, and me up for sports. She had curled and she walked. I swear she was onto the ten-thousand-steps-a-day trend before it was a trend. Curling wasn't my thing, but I did get into running, because Jeannie thought I'd be good at it. And she was right.

Mum always told me that I should play field hockey, too. Appleby started to offer it for girls once I was in grade eight, since more and more of us were registering for the school. A bunch of my friends joined the team, but I was happier playing soccer with the boys. I didn't think it looked like a fun sport, and it was all girls. I think part of me still wanted to be one of the boys. Jeannie was always telling me I'd love field hockey, and she thought I'd be well suited for the sport—I was tall, into running, and I could be pretty aggressive.

A year later, I finally listened to my mum and tried it. I should've done it earlier, because I immediately fell in love with field hockey, and I enjoyed it even more than soccer. Playing on that team was one of the highlights of high school. It was wickedly fun and aggressive. Chasing that ball around the field, seemingly forever. The amazing noise—*thwack!*—when you drilled it off your stick to a teammate. The feeling of putting one past the goalie, and the celebration with your teammates afterward? I loved it all.

Though I wondered: *What's up with the skirts?* It's a badass sport, so it always confused me that we had to play in something delicate-seeming like skirts.

Anyway, we were good. I mean, really good. And finally I felt like I was on a true team in every sense of the word. It wasn't my first team sport by any means, but it was the first team where we played hard for each other. We were possessed to win, practice hard, and have fun. During my time at Appleby, the football team wasn't very good, and neither was the soccer team. The field hockey team was the school's crown jewel. Everybody knew we were good. And I got to be a part of that.

Field hockey made me realize that it wasn't only okay to be aggressive, it was awesome. It's a rough sport and I was rough. I'd come barreling down the field and fire a quick pass to a teammate, then keep going—if you're in my way, look out!—and get the ball back before I fed it to a forward who was heading to the net.

I was by no means our best player, but I was a leader on the team, and I had a voice in the locker room. When I was in grade eleven, we made it to the Ontario high school championship, and again in grade twelve.

I'll never forget that week in November, at my final high school tournament. It was cold and rainy in St. Catharines as we headed to Ridley College. All the visiting teams stayed in a hotel, and we were travelling to and from the field in Sprinter vans. We'd sit in the van, singing, shaking with cold and excitement as we drove to games. And I realized how special this was, even then. No team I had been a part of, either at school or outside of school, felt like a team the way this one did. I swam. Ran. Played tennis. Golfed. But those were all solo sports. With field hockey, there was a togetherness I'd never truly experienced. After every game we'd get into a huddle and we'd sing "Amazing Grace" at the top of our lungs. We'd have our arms around each other, and we'd sway.

"How sweet the sound / That saved a wretch like meeeeee!"

That year in St. Catharines, the game went to penalty strokes—that's what they call penalty shots in field hockey. You don't thwack those, it's more of a flick, kind of like a wrist shot in ice hockey (which I'm still working on, okay?).

Our coach chose me to be one of five players to take a penalty stroke that day. I was a veteran, a senior, and I'd done pretty well when we did penalty strokes in practice. I was so nervous, though. I remember thinking I wanted to be selected. That would mean I was good, right? But at the same time . . . the pressure! Not my favourite. Sweaty, sweaty palms.

One of my teammates went first and she missed. Then it was my turn. I lined up and took a deep breath. Then I flicked the ball and . . . my shot went in! It found the right top corner, luckily. Our team was winning! I got hugs from all my teammates. Our lead didn't last, though. We missed our next one, and the other team scored their next three in a row. And that was it. We lost the game.

It was heartbreaking. I remember feeling so disappointed. We'd come so close to winning. So close to being the best in the province.

We hugged each other so hard in that huddle and we sang "Amazing Grace" like we always did. Some of us had tears in our eyes. It was our last game together, and it hadn't ended the way we'd wanted, but what an experience we'd shared. What a team.

I wish all women especially could have a slice of that, at least once. It taught me loyalty, communication, patience, and how to be a teammate. I think that's something that you need to work on your whole life, whether you play sports or not. I know many girls and teenagers drop sports around the time they get their periods—whether it's because they don't have the confidence, they feel embarrassed, they don't feel they have the skills, or they aren't explicitly invited and included—in any case, it's such a shame.

As I look back at my experiences as a kid, it was field hockey that really got me going in sports. It showed me the collective experience I could have with other girls around my age, and how much fun that is, how powerful it could make us all feel.

I have my mum to thank for my experience. Without Jeannie's push, I never would have played field hockey. I never would've experienced in high school what it feels like to truly be part of a team. To work with other women toward a common goal. To fail and succeed together. To run around on a field in a skirt and feel like an absolute force.

Thanks for the push, Mum.

Something's Wrong

How the heck does anyone drink through the cage of a helmet? I've just sprayed water all over my cheek. So much for staying hydrated while I play hockey. Unclipping my helmet so I can drink seems like a horrible idea. This thing was hard enough to get on in the first place. And don't even get me started on wearing a mouthguard. No one can understand me when I talk with it in my mouth, but trying to reach my hand into my cage to take it out is even more of a catastrophe. Saliva flying. My hand stuck in the cage. Real smooth.

Our first practice at North Toronto Arena has progressed through the warm-up phase, and we've been told to rest and get some water before the drills start. I tried to follow Coach Ethan's instructions . . . and now my cheek is wet.

Coach Ethan is a big guy with a whistle around his neck and a ball cap on his head. He doesn't even wear a helmet on the ice. He's just dumped a bucket full of pucks at centre ice, blown his whistle, and waved us all over. I skate there slowly so I can run out of momentum when I get close. The other women here stop sharply. I stop whatever the opposite of sharply is—dully? Yeah, that's how I stop. I bump ever-so-slightly into one of my team-mates, who pretends not to notice that I need her to help me come to a full stop. That's a kindness. I'll have to get her name and thank her later.

Ethan explains he has us set up to pass back and forth in our first drill. I'm paired with a woman named Angie, who can skate backward and pivot from forward to backward with no trouble. She had no issues getting her gear on. She brought her own jersey. Her stick is clearly cut to a length she likes. She didn't spray herself in the face with water. She hasn't fallen yet. We're in very different phases of our hockey careers.

As my first-ever hockey drill begins, my focus is entirely on get-ting Angie the puck, and awkwardly returning her passes. I'm not doing half bad, either!

Then we go through some shooting drills—I need to figure out how to raise the puck, but Coach Ethan says that'll come with time. "First," he tells me, "you need to work on your aim. Try hitting the net." Okay. Add that to the list of skills I need to pick up. It's early September of my rookie year, 2021, so luckily the season is young. Thank goodness I have time.

By the end of the hour-long skate, I'm covered with sweat. And I'm smiling.

While we're taking our equipment off in the dressing room, a couple of women very kindly tell me, "You didn't do half bad out there!" And "That was awesome for a first practice!" They're sugar-coating things. But I don't mind one bit.

I'm smiling behind my mask as I leave the dressing room, and as I walk out to my car, bag slung over my shoulder, the muscles in my legs are already burning. Those are definitely different ones than

I use in Pilates! I feel so good, and I'm already looking forward to next Tuesday's skate.

I'm about ten minutes from home before my mind returns to something I can only rarely stop thinking about. The reality that hockey was nicely distracting me from. Tears start to fall down my cheeks. I can't stop them.

Nearly a year ago, we started seeing signs that something was wrong with my mum. Back then, they weren't conclusive. But now they're not only signs. It seems like nearly everything about Jeannie has changed. I barely recognize her anymore.

My mum is seventy-two years old, but she never used to be a woman who rested for long during the day. She was always up and running around. Driving into Toronto to see me and George, playing mah-jongg and bridge with her friends, or working in her garden.

But my opinionated, energetic, joyful mum has become . . . empty. That's the best way I can describe her. Jeannie's words have become simple. There is no intonation. No highs. No lows.

She's struggling with simple tasks. She can't put her coffee cup in the microwave because she doesn't have the arm strength to lift her cup. She can walk from the dining room to the living room, and then she sits herself down heavily on the couch for a rest. That's probably the most alarming part: watching Jeannie move. She's so much slower. Less energetic. There's less get-up-and-go, and it's as though she's aged ten years in a couple of months. She sits and watches TV for extended periods of time. My mum never used to do that. The only TV she watched, honestly, was me on Sportsnet. She'd never miss one of my shows.

The first time I noticed something was off with Jeannie was in January of 2021. Mum, George, and I were at a park together. Jeannie met us there, and she had a lot of trouble finding the park, even though I told her the exact address. That was my first clue something was up, because Jeannie drove all the time. She'd travel all over the city looking for the best butcher, the new flower store that was mentioned in the paper, or just to get inspired by the decor and landscaping of other houses. While we were there, she was holding hot chocolates in both hands while we followed George around. While walking, Jeannie hit some uneven ground and fell flat on her face. I mean, *boom*. She hit the ground hard.

It was so awful. Hot chocolate went flying, and there was blood and dirt all over her face. But her reaction wasn't to check herself to to see if she was okay, or to question how she had managed to fall. She didn't check to make sure she still had all her teeth. She didn't cry. She didn't look upset. She didn't ask me where the blood was coming from, even though it was pouring from her nose, and it was all over her hands and face.

But it wasn't like my mum was trying to be tough. It was as though she didn't understand the consequences of the fall or notice any of the blood she was shedding or the pain she was feeling. I, on the other hand, went right into emergency mode. Sat my mum down on the bench. Made sure George was okay. I called Tato and told him what happened, and he immediately hopped in the car and sped over to the park with my sister, Kay.

Thankfully someone at the park saw what happened and asked if I wanted them to run to the fire station that was across the parking lot. "Yes!" I said. I put my arm around my mum, wiped the blood pouring from her nose with her scarf, and continued to talk with her while we waited. George, meanwhile, was happily playing on the jungle gym, unaware of his grandmother's fall.

The firefighters arrived and checked out my mum. I insisted they have the ambulance come. One did, and Jeannie stepped into it like it was no big deal. She was hurt, but she didn't recognize the pain or embarrassment or any of the consequences.

Tato drove to the hospital to be with my mum. They checked for a concussion, but she didn't have one. Her nose wasn't broken, just swollen. She looked awful for the next few days with that swelling and two black eyes.

I still feel tremendous guilt for that fall. If I hadn't come to Oakville that day she wouldn't have fallen. If I had picked a different park that day she wouldn't have fallen. If I hadn't bought the hot chocolates she wouldn't have fallen. And I've been living with that stress and guilt ever since.

Especially because, since that day in the park, the signs Jeannie isn't herself have started to pile up. Tato, Kay, Nick, and I talk about it all the time. "Maybe she's losing her memory," we say. "Maybe it was that fall at the park." We wonder if it's Alzheimer's. Or dementia. After so much isolation, maybe she's just having trouble getting back into the swing of things?

And we're not the only ones noticing that Jeannie is slipping. Fred has been our family's physiotherapist for years, and in March of 2021, during my appointment, a couple months after my mum's fall, he said: "Something's not right with your mom." That was the first time someone outside our family had noticed. That suddenly made it all feel too real.

But after Jeannie goes for a CT scan and an MRI and they both come back fine, we're even more curious and frustrated. My mum is clearly not fine.

"That's good," Jeannie says in response to just about anything these days. "That's good." It's like she's a broken record. And her voice is disappearing, too. She's constantly clearing her throat. We used to talk on the phone all the time, nearly every day. She called me after every single one of my Sportsnet shifts—she'd been doing that for fifteen years. She'd tell me if I was funny, or that she liked my yellow jacket, or wasn't a fan of my hoop earrings. But my mum has stopped calling. And when I call my parents' house, Jeannie doesn't answer.

The friends she loved seeing—she doesn't see them as often anymore, either. She only wants to spend time with family. And when we do see her, Jeannie isn't put together the way she used to be, with a sharp outfit, neat hair, and lipstick. She's wearing the same clothes day after day, and she doesn't look as fresh as she usually is. It's so jarring to see my mum like this.

When a doctor tested her strength this summer, she couldn't lift her arm. Or bend her knees. She couldn't follow her finger as she moved it from left to right. It's clear she's lost her strength—and within the last six months, Jeannie has also lost twenty pounds.

We're watching my mum deteriorate in every way and we don't know why, and we don't know how long she can actually carry on like this. But it's not like Jeannie is angry or upset. She has a good attitude about it all. It's like she doesn't even realize what's been happening to her.

Honestly, that makes it even more frustrating for me. I've always asked my mum for her opinion on everything. Children, work, fashion, cooking, laundry—you name it, she was always my first call. My sounding board. I especially leaned on her when it came to interior design. When Adam and I bought our house in 2015, we did some minor renovations. She was the one dragging me to all the stores for plumbing fixtures, appliances, and drapes. And Jeannie likes to explore every option—she never settles on just one trip to a store.

Jeannie had designed her dream home after Kay, Nick, and I moved out. And so when Adam and I started making plans to tear down and rebuild our house years later to make room for our growing family, she'd given us so much advice and guidance about design ideas. She would spend hours a night going over plans on gridded paper. She'd email me. FaceTime me. Jeannie had so many thoughts: "You should switch the main-floor washroom and closet, because then you'll have more room in the pantry." She convinced us the kitchen island shouldn't include a sink. That the kitchen sink should be set up right below a window. That the ceiling height should be nine feet instead of ten, "because ten-footers are too hard to clean," she said. Jeannie was so full of ideas. She would cut out paper to represent the size of our couch and move it around a proposed future living room in our house, all on that gridded paper.

And now, when I try to talk to her about the house, Jeannie has nothing to say.

"Don't you feel like something's wrong?" I ask her. "You're not yourself." I want her to confess to me or secretly say, "You're right." But she can't understand. She can't compute that something is so, so wrong. She can't articulate that she has changed.

But everything about Jeannie is different. It's like the lights have gone off inside my mum.

I'm nearly home from the rink and my first hockey skills session as I'm replaying all of this in my head. Then I turn my car around and head west to Oakville. I need to see my mum. And I need things to feel as normal as possible.

I try to focus on the music playing in the car during the drive. I'm singing along with Harry Styles's "Watermelon Sugar." But the distraction isn't working. All I'm thinking about is Jeannie.

When I walk through the front door, she's sitting on the light green couch in the living room beside Tato. She has a yellow blanket over her and smiles when she sees me. I smile, too, with tears in my eyes.

I need it to feel like everything is okay. "Mum!" I tell her, holding back tears. "I just had my first skate!"

Jeannie smiles and tells me: "That's good."

It is good. And I'm pretending that my mum is, too. She just has to be.

Team Osmak

"Evanka. That's a cool name."

I'll never forget those words. That's what Wayne Gretzky—the Great One—actually said to twelve-year-old me, back in August of 1993.

It was my brother's sixteenth birthday, and Nick, Kay, Jeannie, Borden, and I were all at the Wayne Gretzky restaurant in downtown Toronto. It had just opened, conveniently located at 99 Blue Jays Way, the perfect home for No. 99. Tato had reserved a special table there to make Nick's sixteenth extra sweet.

A trip to the big city to eat at Gretzky's restaurant was such a treat for us kids. Yes, that same year he'd broken so many hockey fan's hearts in Toronto when he and the LA Kings beat the Maple Leafs in the conference finals, but I'd certainly forgiven the guy. Winning is what great players do, right? And he was giving back to Toronto with this cool restaurant, which had been open only a couple of weeks. Being there was a great way to celebrate Nick's birthday. The chicken wings from Gretzky's restaurant had to be the best around.

At the time, you couldn't have asked for a better sixteenth birthday celebration:

Gretzky—*The Great One*—was actually there at his restaurant. In person.

That's not all. Somehow, sweet-talking Tato convinced No. 99 to come over to our table to wish my brother happy birthday and to meet the whole Osmak family. Gretzky had already won the Stanley Cup four times. He'd won the Art Ross Trophy as the NHL's top point-getter *nine times*. He'd been voted the league MVP nine times, too. And here he was, absolute hockey royalty, standing in front of us, dressed in jeans and a T-shirt, like he was just a regular guy. The Great One was right there!

I pulled a scrap piece of paper and a pen out of Jeannie's purse—she always had exactly what we needed stashed in there. "I'm Evanka," I said, casually as I could manage, when it was my turn to speak to him. That's when Gretzky said those words I'll never forget: "Evanka. That's a cool name." He called me cool! Okay, fine, he called my *name* cool. Still. And then he signed my piece of paper. As I thanked him, I silently vowed to put that autographed paper in a frame as soon as we got home.

He signed a piece of paper for Nick, too. My brother and I were trying to stay calm as Gretzky walked away, but we were high-fiving and trying not to jump up and down and yell with excitement. "Did you see that? The Great One! We met Wayne Gretzky! I got to touch his hand! Maybe some of that Gretzky magic rubbed off on us!" Tato and Jeannie thought it was great to meet Wayne, but it wasn't nearly as cool for them as it was for us. Mum couldn't believe our reaction. "He's just a person," Jeannie told us, shrugging. Ha! *Sure, Mum.* Did Nick or I score 215 points for the Oilers in eighty games during the 1985–86 season? Yeah . . . I don't think so.

My brother and I have the same regret from that memorable

night. Those pieces of paper Gretzky signed for us? Mine never made it into a frame. Neither did Nick's. I'm sure we carefully put those pieces of paper into our pockets or Mum's purse, but I wish we remembered what we'd done with them afterward or how they were lost. Sigh . . . I wonder where they are today.

As kids, we got close to quite a few athletes and went to so many big sporting events. My dad's job gave us a lot of opportunities across every professional sport on offer in Toronto, which I'm so grateful for. But the thing is, as you can probably tell from my parents' somewhat muted reaction to the Great One: Tato and Mum weren't rah-rah sports people, despite all the perks Tato got from his job. They weren't die-hard fans of any team. They didn't ever buy themselves jerseys, though jerseys were usually given to Tato through work. Saturday nights weren't appointment viewing for hockey in our house.

Still, even though Jeannie and Borden didn't watch a ton of sports or play any themselves, they always encouraged us kids to be active. We were a sports family because my parents saw how much joy sports brought their children. As soon as Jeannie noticed that all three of us loved running around and chasing after soccer balls or whacking tennis balls, she signed us up for local teams. Sports may not have been Jeannie's thing, but family was, and we were hers, and she was going to make sure we were enjoying experiences that made us happy. I think cheering us on made her happy, too.

Jeannie had us three years apart: Kay, Nick, then me. We kids were all born in New Jersey, but we moved to Oakville, Ontario, when I was one. Tato had been working on Wall Street in New York and he was promoted to a position in Toronto, so we moved to a smaller city a little west of there.

That's where the memories of my childhood begin, in an Oakville subdivision on Ash Tree Way, a quiet street with tons of families, where most of the houses looked the same. Our street was always the site of sports and action. Kids were running around, playing ball hockey or tag or soccer. I spent many hours on Ash Tree Way kicking footballs to my brother as he practiced receiving. I don't remember being very good with my accuracy or distance, but it was an opportunity for me to improve my kicking, which was key for soccer.

They were terrific athletes, Kay and Nick. Since my sister is six years older than me, we weren't really competitive with each other. We weren't playing the same sports at the same time. For Nick, I was handy to have around so I could help him practice.

My brother was talented, and he went hard. Jeannie would say Nick went *too* hard. There was always a major injury or at least an asthma attack once a season for my brother. In grade ten, he broke a rib and tore a kidney. Took a helmet to the flank while catching a football and missed the rest of the season. I never remember him being down about it, though. Frustrated that he couldn't play anymore, sure, but his poor health never stopped him from competing aggressively or at his top level.

My mum, on the other hand, probably wished he'd been less aggressive. I remember seeing how worried she looked—that furrowed brow—as we watched Nick on the football field. She wasn't thinking about wins and losses; she was just hoping Nick and his teammates walked off the field uninjured. I now understand the reason for her worry as I watch George and Blake bump around sports fields. I'm not going to lie—sometimes I have to hold my breath or even look away while five-year-old Blake is running full tilt at another kid, trying to get that soccer ball. Or as eight-year-old George is flying down the ice, chasing after a puck. There isn't a sport George doesn't play.

It was the same for my sister and brother and I. We were always ripping around on Ash Tree Way. The three of us tried basically every sport you could play. Summer weekends were spent playing, but also enjoying our neighbourhood in so many other ways. We'd have street-wide garage sales, we'd carpool to different events with our neighbours, have pizza parties in somebody's basement that looked the same as ours. It was a cozy childhood, in large part because my mum made it so: Jeannie was the master of having chips and enough snacks if an impromptu party broke out at our place, always making everyone feel welcome. Mum was an effortless entertainer that way, because she loved to be around people, and would chat up a storm about anything and everything.

I'll never forget the street-wide party that broke out when one of our family station wagons died in the summer of 1986 and had to be put to pasture. Our family always had station wagons. Blue. Green. Red. The forest-green one was most famous, known in our neighbourhood as "the Beast on the Street." The thing was LOUD. Maybe it had a muffler issue? Who knows. But when we finally had to say goodbye to the old Beast, all our neighbours came out to watch it get towed, and they clapped as it rolled off. Then we had a street-wide pizza party, organized by none other than Jeannie. It was a perfect going-away party for the Beast on the Street. All of us were sure going to miss that booming noise from our family vehicle. The Beast was part of the neighbourhood, part of our tight-knit community's lore.

Since most of the kids on the street were older, like my brother's and sister's ages, I spent a lot of time trying to keep up. I never really noticed that most of the kids I played with were five or six years older than me. I mean, I noticed, but I guess it never mattered to me. I'd play dress-up with Kay and her friends. I absolutely loved sporting jewels and running around pretending I was Madonna, singing into a hairbrush microphone. I loved the independence and feeling like I was older and elegant. Often I'd throw on one of my mum's dresses that didn't fit me at all, or put on her necklaces and bracelets and walk around on my tiptoes. My mum was fancy and always put together, and I noticed that from a young age. I wanted to be fancy, too.

We Osmaks spent a lot of time together, and we were a close crew. Tato was an only child, so the idea of a big family was something sacred to him. And Jeannie made sure we spent lots of time together, and planned family trips every year. My parents loved having the five of us all together. Road trips in the Beast and our future station wagons were huge for our crew, as were trips in general. Mum and Tato didn't travel much as kids, and they wanted to give us that experience when they could.

We'd load up in the car and head south, usually. To South Carolina. Or Florida. Or out west to Manitoba, where my mum's from. She liked to visit her mom as often as she could, and battling the black flies in Manitoba in the summer was a lot easier than dealing with the frigid temperatures in the winter.

To break up the trips, we'd always have a sports component. We'd hit up a hall of fame. Or a stadium. Or go see a game or two. Some families go to galleries and museums, but ours didn't. Our tourism experience incorporated sports instead. And even though my parents weren't avid fans, they knew their kids were, and they knew we'd enjoy seeing stadiums and games in different cities.

We stopped one year at Michigan University in Ann Arbor to see the football stadium—the Big House. It seats more than one hundred thousand people. I'd never been in a crowd that big, and I remember walking in and saying: "Holy smokes. This is WAY bigger than the SkyDome!" You couldn't fit half that crowd in the stadium where the Jays played. It was unbelievable to me. And for college sports? I just couldn't wrap my head around it. It was so cool to see the biggest stadium in the US in person.

In 1990 we headed to Chicago and saw the White Sox stadium, the old Comiskey Park, being demolished. It was the oldest professional baseball park in operation. I remember talking to Nick about how sad it was to see all those excavators going to work. Wasn't this an important part of history, after all? Tato told us it was being torn down to make way for a new, state-of-the-art stadium.

We also visited South Bend Indiana, to check in on the University of Notre Dame football facilities, where the Fighting Irish played. Nick was blown away walking in. He pictured himself playing there in the future, wearing one of those iconic green jerseys. This was all before my brother hurt himself playing football. It was 1993, the year the movie *Rudy* came out. A scrappy kid who wasn't the best at football earning his way onto the Fighting Irish roster. It immediately became my brother's favourite movie.

That same year, we Osmaks started to become a basketball family. Thanks to his work with the Bank of Nova Scotia, Tato was one of the founding directors of the Toronto Raptors basketball club when the franchise joined the National Basketball Association for the 1995–96 season.

For as many amazing sporting events we got to see as kids, Kay, Nick, and I were more up close and personal with the Toronto Raptors than with any other team. We basically had an inside track, and that was all thanks to our dad.

Our whole family attended the first-ever Raptors game at what was then called the SkyDome on November 3, 1995, in a crowd of just over thirty thousand fans. Because the Dome wasn't set up for basketball, about half the seats were permanent and half were bleachers they'd rolled in. But it didn't feel temporary or makeshift. Fans were so loud in welcoming this team to the city.

I'll never forget the pregame show. Just before they introduced the starting lineup, this huge spotted egg was wheeled out to centre court. I remember looking at Nick and Nick looking at me and both of us wondering what the heck was going on. And then suddenly the egg started to break open like it was hatching. And out popped a big red plush Raptor mascot, sporting basketball shoes and a team jersey with No. 95, for the team's inaugural year. We absolutely lost it. He was perfect! Professional basketball had arrived in Toronto, and it was amazing.

The Raptors won that first game, beating the New Jersey Nets, 94–79. It was unreal, and I figured the winning would continue all season long. Boy, was I ever wrong.

The summer after the Raptors' inaugural season, in 1996, we hit the road for another Osmak family trip. This time to Atlanta, and with a purpose—it was the site of the Summer Olympics that year. And—can you believe this?—we got to see the Dream Team. I'm talking Charles Barkley, David Robinson, Grant Hill, Shaq, Karl Malone . . . Just an unbelievable roster. Our seats were so far away that we didn't actually see much of that game, but to say I was there is pretty cool. We also saw Olympic European handball and volley-ball. That was my introduction to handball as a sport. It was so fast! And the volleyball players absolutely hammered those balls. It was awesome, and my first experience at the Olympics.

We Osmaks always worked in a sporting event or a visit to a major sports venue during our road trips, which meant we also spent a lot of time in the car getting to our various destinations. And we had to keep ourselves entertained, right? This was before we had a CD player in the car, definitely before Bluetooth, well before the days of iPads playing movies to keep the kids occupied in the back seat. The three of us kids were on the bench seat, and when we weren't singing, usually Kay was reading and Nick was quizzing me on sports. He would say: "Name all thirty-two NFL teams!" and I'd rattle them off. "How fast can you list the American League and National League teams?" I'd rip through those MLB teams quick as I could. And then Nick was onto the next question. We were both sports-crazed, so I was more than happy to partici-pate. I never knew how much my brother's sports quizzes would prepare me for my eventual career.

We laugh about it now: Nick definitely wanted a brother, so I was basically his puppet. I wasn't what you'd call a total jock—I loved Barbies, loved putting on Jeannie's lipstick, loved admiring fancy women with nice hair and clothes. But I also loved sports. And for that, Nick was thankful. We grew close because we played and talked sports a lot.

And those road trips were full of talking. Have you ever been in a station wagon with four other people for sixteen hours, pre-phones? So we talked. Mum was always in the front, often laughing. Jeannie was a cheap, easy laugh, and always had a twinkle in her eye. She was always up for something fun, like a game of I Spy if she could tell we were getting bored.

Years later, it was Mum who drove me and my friends Lara and Ainsley to South Carolina one March break, where we stayed for a week. We sang and laughed the whole car ride there. We barbecued great meals. The three of us got closer because my mum decided we should include my best friends on the trip. As I write this, it occurs to me that Lara and Ainsley remain two of my best friends because of those experiences we had as kids. And they're two of my favourite people to be around, to this day. My mum helped cultivate some of these earliest friendships.

Lara and I bonded initially over our shared love of sports, and it's the thread that has run through our friendship since day one. And listen, I recognized from a young age that I wasn't going pro. I was not the next Christine Sinclair on the soccer field, scoring a boatload of goals and winning Olympic gold—this much was sadly, glaringly clear. Quite a shame, because I knew I wanted to be around that feeling big games and sports created. But I found other ways to get closer to the action.

I played tennis as a kid, and I'll never forget the first time I saw ball kids working at a big provincial tournament. They were running around the court, at lightning speed, then stopping on a dime, and suddenly they were ready in a flash to throw a tennis ball to a big-name player. I said to my mum: "One day, I'm going to be a ball kid!"

When I was old enough, Jeannie sought out that opportunity for me. She signed me up to be a ball kid when I was eleven and I actually got to work at that provincial tournament. I loved everything about it. Seeing the players up close. Running as fast as I could across the net to collect a ball that hadn't made it over. Throwing a ball to a great player and having her throw it right back if she felt it was flat, or just wanted another one. I learned some players' superstitions: Some would only accept new balls from a specific side of the court. I learned who needed their towel after every serve because they got super sweaty. I could relate to that one! And watching them serve—the power of their shots was incredible! Seeing them rip crosscourt winners or perfectly locate their drop shots. And then the celebrations on court after they won—those were the best. I loved being around that energy.

The biggest sporting event I worked as a kid was in August of 1994, and it was packed with that type of energy. Nick and I were ball kids at the International Basketball Federation (FIBA) World Championships, which were held in Toronto at the SkyDome and Maple Leaf Gardens, and in Hamilton at Copps Coliseum.

All three locations were a pretty easy drive from our family home, and Jeannie was more than happy to drive me and Nick. Always while playing her nearly worn-out Melissa Etheridge CD, turning the volume way up for "Come to My Window." Mum always listened to music in the car when she drove us kids around. She'd blast Rita MacNeil on tape and later CD. She'd play the same tunes over and over. I knew all the words to "Flying on Your Own" before I'd turned ten.

At these FIBA World Championships—shuttled back and forth by my mum, and fuelled by Rita MacNeil—I got a very up-close look at the action. Unlike my experience a few years later in Atlanta, when I got to see the Dream Team, this time I saw Shaq from just feet away. And oh my goodness . . . seeing that guy in person was intimidating, to say the least. Shaquille O'Neal is seven foot one and more than three hundred pounds. I could barely keep it together when I had to pass him a ball during the warm-up. I felt like he needed a bigger ball to play with than his teammates!

Shaq was all smiles during the warm-up. Joking around with his teammates. Slamming the ball into the basket here and there. I watched him drink water and thought to myself that his hand could've wrapped around the bottle twice. I could tell his teammates loved him, too. Shaq got a lot of pats on the back and high fives from the other guys on the court with him.

Shaq caught my eye, but I had an important job to do. Getting these guys basketballs during breaks in play, or while they were warming up. I worked five games that week, but when Team USA won the final against Russia and Shaq was named MVP, I wasn't working. I hadn't been picked. I was super disappointed, and I had no idea how they picked the final ball kids, but I definitely wanted to be one of them. I watched the final on TV, and I much preferred my front-row, in-person seat. Nick didn't work the final, either, which made me feel better. "You two did a great job!" Mum told us. "They probably went with more experienced kids."

Maybe. But either way, I realized my future career probably wasn't as a ball kid. Still, working games at that world championship showed me yet again that I felt such energy around sports; in this case, being on the court. It made me realize I needed to be in sports forever.

A few years after I threw Shaq those basketballs, I graduated from high school, part of Appleby's class of 1998. I was so excited to be done with high school because my life was all set: I'd made my career decision. I'd chosen my path.

If you'd asked me my favourite thing back then as I was about to head off to Queen's University, I wouldn't have hesitated for a second. It was sports. (Boys and candy were probably tied for second.)

But I was doing what I thought I was supposed to do. The responsible thing. Something my parents, and particularly my mum, who'd studied physics and math, would be proud of.

I had decided to study . . . engineering.

Looking back, I wonder why I veered so far off course back then. Why I strayed so far from the love of my life. Because the career I'd planned for myself had nothing at all to do with sports.

Or so I thought.

Reality

There couldn't possibly be enough concealer in the world to cover the circles under my eyes. It was Tuesday, September 21, 2021, and I was at Sportsnet's studios in downtown Toronto, sitting in the makeup chair, at about six p.m. My body was there, sure. But I was basically a robot.

I felt drained. I wasn't sleeping well. I was crying a lot.

Being at work had been my escape from reality. Where I could just be on autopilot and not have to think about what was happening in my life. I could focus on games. Talk about players. Even have some laughs.

That day, Ken told me a story about his weekend, and I was listening as best I could. "I birdied seventeen, and then you won't believe what happened on the last hole. I fell apart!" He was going through his round of golf, but I wasn't firing back quick jabs about how obviously he fell apart because he sucks at golf, or laughing or asking for more details like I usually would. I didn't have it in me. Nadine, my makeup artist, probably thought I pulled an all-nighter or had a few bottles of wine the night before. If only I looked this tired because I'd been having a good time.

Ken didn't know. I hadn't told Nadine, either. I didn't feel ready to tell any friends what was happening in my life. I knew if I even started talking about my mum, I'd start crying, and I wouldn't be able to stop. I felt too fragile. And Nadine could only apply so much foundation and waterproof mascara. Crying on air was not an option.

Plus, I figured that if I told any friends about what was happening in my life, I'd have to acknowledge that it was real. And I wasn't prepared to accept that.

A couple of weeks earlier, in September of 2021, my family had started to get answers about what was wrong with my mum. It was the news none of us wanted to hear. Jeannie had seen a doctor just outside of Toronto, since her ability to speak had worsened and her arm strength was deteriorating—she couldn't raise an arm. Based on these symptoms and after seeing her in person, the doctor referred her to a clinic at McMaster University in Hamilton that specializes in ALS.

ALS. That was the first time we'd heard those three letters applied to my mum. It wasn't on our radar at all. No one had mentioned it before that visit. Those letters stand for amyotrophic lateral sclerosis. It was an absolute bombshell.

I knew ALS was also known as Lou Gehrig's disease, but I wasn't sure what exactly ALS was. I just knew it wasn't good.

The only time ALS had really existed in my world was during the Ice Bucket Challenge that went viral. Remember that? It was around 2014. If you were challenged by someone online, you had to dump a bucket of ice over your head and then challenge three other people to do the same. I did it, too. But I think I cheated. I'm not even sure

I used ice. Anyway, I never would have connected that with what my mum was going through.

When I googled ALS, it was immediately apparent there was no good outcome. I couldn't even cry in that moment because it was all so foreign to me, and it didn't make sense. My family had always assumed that my mum would be around well after she turned one hundred, because Jeannie's own mom had lived an incredible life until the age of 102. My baba—grandma—Elizabeth was living alone and was totally with it until she was ninety-nine. We figured Jeannie might even outlast us all. And yet here we were, facing a reality in which my mum might not make it to her seventy-third birthday.

How had this energetic woman with incredible genes developed this disease?

What I discovered in my Google searches was that my mum's body would shut down completely. That the nerve cells in her brain and spinal cord that control voluntary muscle movement and breathing would stop working. She'd stop walking. Talking. Chewing. Breathing. No treatment stops or reverses ALS. I read all that in about three paragraphs, and that was more than enough information for me. I slammed my laptop shut.

I couldn't accept this news. None of us could.

If my mum had ALS, this was a death sentence.

And so Tato, Kay, Nick, and I did the only thing we could: We held on to disbelief, and we held on hard. It was all we had. *Could it really be?* we wondered. No, it couldn't. And since the clinic in Mississauga hadn't confirmed a diagnosis, we could hold out hope that the fine doctors at the ALS clinic would tell us that my mum's referral had been a mistake.

But when Jeannie and Borden visited that Hamilton clinic with Kay, who had accompanied them to be an extra advocate and ear, our hope was completely shattered.

My sister and parents called me on the way home from McMaster. Kay and Borden were the ones telling me the news, but they weren't crying. Their voices were even-toned, relaying everything the doctor had told them.

"She has ALS," Kay told me. "We're hoping for the best, that it progresses as slowly as possible."

And that was basically it, plus a whole lot of silence on my end. The conversation was short, and it was everything I could do to keep it together. To keep my voice steady as I said: "Goodbye. I love you all."

Then I sobbed. About an hour later, I called Kay back and I asked her every question I had.

How long will mum be with us? How much time do we have left together?

How long will it take for her body to shut down?

How did this happen to our mum when we have no family history of this disease?

But there were no answers. Not to any of my questions.

I couldn't even cry into the phone, and I didn't want to. I was in shock, even though I knew deep down that something devastating like this was probably coming. Now it was here.

I hung up with my sister and that's when I started sobbing. Talking to myself and shaking my head in disbelief.

Why is this happening? I thought. *Why? Why? No! It can't be true!*

Jeannie didn't have much of a reaction to the diagnosis—she didn't have much reaction to anything in those days. Tato was quiet, probably in denial. Kay was crying regularly, and Nick was trying to keep it together for the rest of us, I think. I didn't want to talk to my brother or sister about it anymore, after I'd called Kay with those unanswerable questions. Talking about the diagnosis just made it too real for me.

Luckily, I didn't have to work that night because it was a Thursday, so I could stay home with George and Blake. The boys who Jeannie loved to no end. The boys Jeannie spoiled. The boys Jeannie would never get to see grow up.

She was a professional grandma, or "Nama," as they called her. That started with my sister Kay's eldest, Elizabeth, who couldn't say "Nana," and said "Nama" instead, so it stuck. Blake was only a year and a half, so he couldn't quite talk yet—he just yelled various sounds at her. It worked. She talked to him like they had their own language. "Ba!" he'd yell. "Baaaa!" my mum would yell back, laughing. "Are you a sheep, Blakey?"

Jeannie was already being robbed at this point. Robbed of picking the boys up, robbed of running around with them. And with COVID still rampant, restrictions were on-again, then off-again, depending on where you lived. Our interactions were already so limited.

Adam heard me on the phone with my family and he was right there listening. He did his best to comfort me, both of us in disbelief. But what could he say? What could anyone say? I wanted to call my mum and cry. I wanted to hug her and reverse what I had just heard. I wanted to turn back time and have one more day with my vibrant, fun, energetic mum. But I couldn't. None of us could.

It was official: Jeannie was dying. My mum was disappearing before our eyes.

It was four days after we got all that news that I held it together on air for my shift at Sportsnet. Ken and I had plenty to report on, and I was thankful for the distraction. The Major League Baseball wild-card race was heating up. Training camps were underway ahead of the upcoming NHL season: Would the Tampa Bay Lightning be able to pull off an incredible three-peat? How much closer would Alex Ovechkin get to Gretzky's all-time record of 894 goals? Could Connor McDavid improve on last season's incredible 105 points?

I smiled. I even laughed. I joked around with Ken on air. I focused on my job.

When the show was over, just before three a.m., I walked straight out of the building. I got into my black SUV. As I put the keys into the ignition and settled into my seat, the radio was tuned to 99.9 and I sobbed along with Kelly Clarkson or Ed Sheeran, I can't remember which.

I cried for fifteen minutes before I could see well enough to drive myself home.

The tears slowed down, but they fell for the entire twenty-five-minute drive.

It's lonely enough being one of the only cars on the road in the wee hours of the morning. It was also the only time I could be truly alone with my thoughts and my questions. And I didn't want to be alone with my thoughts and questions. I had too many negative thoughts, too many sad questions with no answers—or with downright horrible answers.

I got home and I cried myself to sleep.

Work in Progress

’ve been known to pull a one-eighty. To make decisions other people might say come way out of left field. To take risks I don't consider risky, or rather, make a decision without considering all the risks. It's why people who know me well aren't shocked when I try something new.

I like to live in left field. It's exciting out here. I think part of that is because I grew up with a mum who went her own way. Who decided when she was sixteen that she wasn't going to be a farmer, so she travelled more than two thousand kilometres east to see what else was out there.

And while I didn't pick up and move across the country or take a massive risk when I decided on my path after high school, my decision to become an engineer did come out of left field.

I really did take Mum and Tato (pleasantly) by surprise when I told them I wanted to study engineering in university. The way I saw it, Borden had a steady job his whole life, worked in the same field his whole career, and my parents surely expected the same from me. So they were a little shocked and very excited when I told them about my future as an engineer. They were probably expecting I'd do something with a sports angle. But engineering, they said, seemed like a great career.

I sure hoped so. Because I had no idea what an engineer actually did.

The way I came to the decision was pretty simple. After our field hockey season wrapped up when I was in grade twelve, I was starting to get my university applications ready. I'd been hunting down the guidance counsellor, Dr. Pierce. I wondered what I should major in, what school would be the right fit. Dr. Pierce's approach to finding those answers was to ask what I was studying. Since I'd been doing a lot of science and math—just like my mum did at that same age—he told me that engineering was a career that incorporates both. Perfect. Decision made. Future set. What a piece of cake.

I liked that it sounded like an impressive degree, too. That it was tough didn't scare me—it excited me. None of my friends were going into engineering, but I didn't care about that. I figured I'd make friends. That engineering was a male-dominated field didn't give me pause, either. I'd had my experience as one of the first girls admitted to Appleby College, so I could navigate a male-dominated field. Easy peasy. Mum did that in the sixties when she went to university, for Pete's sake. And let's be serious: The thought of being in a male-dominated program in university was amazing to nineteen-year-old me. The odds of meeting a guy I liked were in my favour. Maybe a nerdy engineer type.

Maybe it was a good thing that I didn't stop to think too much about being in the minority; I think I've been lucky that I've made some big decisions in my life despite what others are doing or saying. My general approach in life has been: Do I want to go around the brick wall or dig a hole and crawl under it? Neither: I'll punch straight through. For so much of my life, I've been pushing against a giant glass ceiling. Engineering just seemed like a way to keep pushing that glass.

And while I was becoming an engineer, I wanted to party. I wanted to have fun. I love socializing, I love friends, and I wanted the full university experience. I had decided Queen's University was the place for me, in Kingston, Ontario, a school that could offer the social experience I wanted while I worked toward my degree.

So let's go! I thought. *Let's have the best time. Let's get after it!*

I did. I also failed two courses my first semester. And put on fifteen pounds, maybe more. By the end of first year, I'd put on twenty. I guess I had the full university experience, right?

Seriously, though, I can joke about it now, but at the time, I was devastated. I felt like a failure. I'd been at the top of my class at Appleby, and a good field hockey player. I didn't play any sports at Queen's because I was focused on what I knew would be a demanding program. Engineering, plus fitting in all the partying I had to do—*had to do*—seemed like it would be more than enough on my plate for year one.

I was terrified to tell my parents I'd failed two midterm tests just ahead of Thanksgiving because I was scared of disappointing them. I'd always sought their approval. But I picked up the phone and called, and luckily Jeannie and Borden were understanding.

Mum, in particular, was surprisingly okay. She was the first in her immediate family to attend university, and look what I'd done! I was worried I was going to get reamed out.

"It's okay," Mum said. "It happened, and it's done. Just try harder next semester."

It was exactly what I needed to hear. And my mum knew it, because both of my parents realized how upset I was about it. They knew I was disappointed in myself, and piling on with criticism wasn't going to help.

And maybe this was the kick in the pants I needed to really focus. I decided I wasn't giving up on engineering just because I'd stumbled out of the gate. I knew I wasn't destined to be a great engineer, but I was going to stick with it. I was going to become a decent engineer. How's that for dreaming big?

In the middle of first year, we had to declare our discipline within the field. I chose civil engineering because I thought it might be the best path for my skill set. I'd thought about focusing on mining for a brief period, but the idea of moving north and never seeing the sun didn't strike me as a good time. So civil it was. I had met Betsy, who would go on to become a good friend of mine, at the make-up class for kids who failed. She was pursuing civil, too. That was a bonus.

The gender mix in that discipline was probably about 60 per cent male, 40 per cent female, which I liked. I had a good group of girlfriends. We'd study together and we'd also go on pub crawls. A healthy balance, if you ask me.

I didn't fail a class after that first semester. I graduated university with average grades, and a few months before I was done, I'd already lined up a job at Charlton Engineering in Mississauga.

I was twenty-one years old with a ring on my right pinkie that I'd earned because I was an engineer. I was about to start my super-steady and impressive career. I was proud of myself. Jeannie and Borden were proud of me, too.

"Congratulations, Evanka—we knew you could do it," Mum

told me, grinning. "You're about to start a new chapter of your life. It's so exciting!"

I'd still be living at home, since the firm I was working for wasn't too far from Oakville. What also drew me to Charlton was that the company specialized in building homes and subdivisions and planning roads and community layouts. I liked the design aspect of engineering. My mum definitely had a lot of influence on me when it came to design. She was always reading magazines about home style, pointing out aspects of neighbour's gardens that she wanted to try out in her own, or returning from a store with an idea for a new paint colour in the living room. Jeannie was always designing, and she loved it. I wasn't as passionate about design as my mum was, but she got me thinking about how things were laid out and presented, which was useful in my first engineering job.

I started a week after I graduated. I was excited to hit the ground running and get going with my lifelong career.

The company was run by Russ and Andre, and there were just five of us in the office. My job was to be junior to Andre, who mostly dressed in black turtlenecks and sleek pants. His wife, Grace—a petite woman with flaming-red hair—worked in the office, too. Andre and Grace were so kind to me, and really took me under their wing. We were a small crew, but despite their kindness, we never quite had the camaraderie in the office that I expected and craved. I was the youngest employee by twenty or more years. There was no gossiping at the water cooler or spending time together out of the office. And because of our location on the outskirts of Mississauga, there wasn't an opportunity to meet other professionals in the area.

Day to day, my job was a mix of checking on existing projects and trying to secure new ones. I'd be putting together bids for potential developments. Several firms, including ours, would compete to win the contract with a landowner to take on a big job, like designing a suburb. I'd itemize everything we'd need for the job. How much soil would need to be moved? What was the design flow for a sanitary sewer? Where would the mailboxes go?

As engineers, we got price estimates from various tradespeople who were involved with things like surveying the land, excavating, and laying the asphalt. We'd choose the most economical and efficient option. Say a developer bought five acres from a farmer that he wanted to develop: He would give the land to a consultant, like our firm, and we'd come up with a plan that would have to be approved by the municipality, and then we'd put it out for tender, and invite other companies to bid to provide the services.

We'd work on things like tree removal, flattening of land, cutting for roadways. We'd base our decision on price, timing, and reputation. As a small firm, we couldn't put out too many contracts, since we couldn't handle too many at a time. Once the package of quotes was complete, we would submit it to either the municipality or the developer for approval. Sometimes we won the bid and other times we came up short. But we won more than we lost. Since I'd put so much time and energy into putting bids together, sure, I hoped we'd win a few. But would I be devastated if we didn't? Nah. I was always busy.

When we had secured a bid, I'd calculate the amount of soil needed, the design and flow of the sanitary and storm sewers, the slope of the lot for drainage purposes. I'd do everything that went into the design aspects. I wouldn't call it glamourous work. My brain hurts now even thinking about some of the calculations that would be in my inbox every day.

We built big subdivisions in Mississauga. In Orangeville. In Brampton. Much of my job was driving around to different sites, showing up in a white hard hat and brown steel-toed boots, making sure the slopes were correct, that all the calculations had been followed to plan. I will proudly report that sewage never leaked where it shouldn't have. I nailed that planning—shit didn't go everywhere! Success.

But I didn't *love* any aspect of my job. I saw how much my mum loved planning and design, how much she loved talking to people about it, and I wished I had that kind of passion for what I was doing. I just didn't feel enthusiastic enough about any aspect of my job.

When my parents were building their house, Mum knew every contractor's name, even if Doug was only in there for an hour or two to do some grouting in the bathrooms. And day to day, she knew the butcher she'd go to for specific meats, and that butcher would save Jeannie's favourite cut for her, and knew her by name. She'd ask about his kids, and Jeannie knew their names, too. There was a florist named Frank who'd do anything for my mum, and always knew when she was heading in there that she'd be asking for hydrangeas or, depending on the time of year, what she'd be looking for. Frank knew my mum's favourite colour was white. My mum had relationships with all of these people, and I wished I could have cultivated that at my job when I was going to various sites.

But I truly didn't like it enough, and I didn't have the genuine curiosity to ask questions and remember names and talk enthusiastically about the work. I wanted to get in, do the job, and get out and go home.

Looking back, I should've talked more to my parents about

being unhappy at work. Mum would've been the one I would have gone to. But I think I believed that as much as I admired her and valued my parents' opinions, I was building up a little bit of courage to do things my own way. So it didn't cross my mind to consult with them. Plus, I don't think they would've given me a direction I wanted to hear.

I did like parts of my work, like seeing the transformation, watching a subdivision slowly appear. But the planning and calculations? No thank you. And that was most of my job, which made going to work feel like a chore. On Sunday nights I'd wonder: *How am I going to get through this week?* I not only didn't love my job, I barely liked it. It didn't help that I felt like I was okay at it, and not great. I was basically just getting by.

One day I was driving to a site and listening to sports talk radio. The hosts were talking about Augusta National, the course where the Masters is held, which at the time didn't allow female members. I was a member at a Mississauga golf course; I called in to relay my experience as a female player, and the station took my call live on air. I was so nervous that my voice was shaking. But I told them all about the restrictions for women at my club: We couldn't play at certain times and weren't even allowed into one of the course's pubs—that was for men only. I was a junior, so I paid less, and women paid lesser fees than men, but it was ridiculous. Archaic and unfair. There was one woman who fought it and said she'd pay the men's fees so she could play the men's hours. I don't know what came of that. I told them on the radio that I wanted to play golf any time I was free. And I wanted to go to that pub. I'm really good at drinking!

I detailed all this, and the hosts thanked me for my call. I couldn't believe it: I'd just been on air! And no, I wasn't sitting there thinking it would be the first of many times for me. It wasn't an *aha* moment. But those car rides were some of the most fun parts of my job as an engineer, because I didn't have to do my actual job.

In January of 2004, I decided I couldn't keep living this way. I wasn't enjoying my life. I interviewed at a different engineering firm because I wondered if maybe I was just in the wrong role, but I knew from the interview process that the firm wasn't my problem. I wasn't excited about engineering.

It was my boyfriend at the time, Paul, who encouraged me to think outside the box. He sure had. Paul's father was a successful lawyer, and Paul had been expected to take over the family business. But he loved basketball, and he'd decided to pursue coaching. We'd been dating on and off through high school and had started dating again late in university. I was so proud of him for following his passion and taking a path his family didn't expect, but one that made him happy.

I'll never forget the way Paul phrased the question about how I should figure out what I'd do next. He asked: "If you were on a different planet with no expectations from other people, no preconceived notions of who you are and what you should be doing, what would you pursue for the love of it?"

I had been thinking a lot about my mum and dad and what they would say. What would they think? I knew Tato and Jeannie were proud of me for having the career I'd carved out for myself.

But when Paul asked what I'd pursue for the love of it, I immediately thought of the meteorologist I watched on our local station. Weather wasn't an interest of mine, but I loved her confidence on camera and how comfortable she was interviewing people. I pictured myself speaking to the camera, in front of bright lights, looking polished. My nails would always be perfect. My posture in the chair would be great as I informed the thousands of people watching me on TV about everything they needed to know. That seemed like such a cool job. And an impressive job. That's what I wanted for myself.

When I was watching TV on my own or with family at home, it was usually sports. But I'd be watching games. I wasn't one of those kids who was glued to the TV sports highlights, or reading the morning newspaper to check scores or stats. The way I got my sports news was from the radio. I'd listen to Bob McCown every day on The Fan 590 while I drove home from my engineering job. He was the biggest voice in sports at the time, and I hung on to his every word. I wouldn't get out of the car until his show was done. I remember sitting there listening while Bob interviewed a local reporter in Akron, Ohio, about a young high school basketball phenom named LeBron James, and they were talking about how there was no ceiling on this young talent. I stayed in the car for at least fifteen minutes after I got home so I didn't miss any of that conversation. Jeannie and Borden had even started listening to Bob, because I told them how great the show was. Bob didn't suffer fools. He gave great interviews. He had knowledge across all sports. I was hooked.

So I knew I loved TV. I knew I loved sports. And that's what I wanted to cover.

I told Paul, "I would love to be a sports reporter on TV." And he said, "Then figure out how to do that."

And that was it. I didn't need permission to leave engineering or follow my passion, but getting that acceptance from someone who knew me was a big help.

The next phase went into motion quickly. Once I had decided I was leaving engineering, it was a done deal—at least in my head. But I hadn't given my two weeks' notice. I was going to wait until I had a plan in place before I did that. So I put all my attention into finding a journalism school to go to. I had zero skills or experience and no connections in the media world. I figured going back to school was the only way to gain that.

I knew this would all be a very unpleasant surprise to my parents. I would be surprised, too, if I were them. Here I was leaving a stable, professional career for something that had seemingly come out of thin air. But I knew I wanted to give this a go. And heck, both of my parents had taken right turns during their lives to arrive where they did: Jeannie left the farm behind, and Borden dropped out of law school and later pursued an MBA instead. So I was following in their footsteps, right?

I did a Google search of all the schools in the Toronto area that offered broadcasting programs. I knew I didn't want to move out of my parents' house because renting a place would cost money, and if I was going to go back to school, I'd need to save wherever I could. And I wasn't keen on taking a multiple-year program, especially if I didn't turn out to be very good at it.

Given my strict parameters, I had no idea what to expect. But after two days of scouring the web, it appeared: a four-month-long journalism program at Seneca College at York University.

Okay, this was doable. I didn't have to move away from home, and it was only for the summer.

I'm not one to wait once I make a decision. I told my parents the plan that night in the kitchen. Jeannie tried her best to look supportive. "See how the summer goes," she kept saying with a tight smile on her face.

"I'm paying for the program, and if it doesn't work out, I can always go back to engineering," I told them over and over. That was my pitch. I had saved enough money from engineering and living at home to take the summer off. I figured that would make my decision easier for Jeannie and Borden to swallow.

I'll never forget what Tato said: "You're leaving behind a stable career—a profession—to chase a cockamamie dream." And: "You've never acted before." He kept shaking his head angrily.

I tried to explain to Borden that reporting on sports isn't acting. That I'd be a serious sports reporter discussing serious games with serious consequences in the world of sports fans. But Borden wasn't buying it. He didn't hide the fact he thought my plan was an awful pipe dream. I was hurt by that. I was twenty-four and I wondered, *Why don't you trust me to make a sound decision? And trust that I'm trying it for the summer? And most of all, what's wrong with seeing what else is out there?*

My mum was more understanding, which I appreciated. Probably because she figured I'd return to my stable career soon after dabbling in journalism.

I did recognize my parents' concern, since this was a complete departure from my last career, and a bit of a head-scratcher.

Borden just couldn't understand the one-eighty I was pulling. So I reminded him, "It's only a summer break. I can always go back to my good old steady career." No matter how many times I repeated, "It's just a summer off!" I couldn't convince Tato. He was not pleased. But my mind was made up.

The next day, I asked the guys at the engineering firm for the summer off. I left it open-ended, and said I was going to try out broadcasting, "just for a few quick months." I asked if there would still be a job for me if I were to return after the summer, and luckily they assured me the job would be waiting. They didn't say anything to my face, but I'm sure they thought I was absolutely insane. That didn't bother me one bit.

Very early on, I knew that going back to school had not been a mistake. Four days into the journalism program at Seneca, it was clear it wasn't just a summer fling. I didn't tell my parents right away, but I was hooked. I loved speaking to the camera. I loved reporting. I loved interviewing people. I loved learning how to edit tapes. I loved writing scripts. I loved trying to figure out what colours really popped on TV when it came to my wardrobe.

I knew I'd never go back to engineering. For me, engineering was like farm life had been for Jeannie. We just didn't fit. Mum had to get off the farm and I had to get out of the firm.

Those four months at Seneca flew by. The idea of going back to my old job actually made me feel sick. I called Andre and thanked him for the opportunity to work at his firm, but I let him know engineering wasn't for me. He was shocked—I think he figured I'd definitely be back after the summer. But he wished me well and said: "Hope I see you on TV someday!" I hoped so, too.

Surprisingly, Jeannie and Borden didn't seem too upset that I wasn't going right back to my engineering job. But I think they held on to hope that I'd go back to my steady career after giving journalism a try. Hey, it's a tough industry, I don't blame them for doubting me! I would've, too.

I don't know what I expected after graduating from Seneca; I guess part of me thought I'd land a job easily and quickly with all my experience. All four months of it. It took time, and I was constantly looking for opportunities anywhere and everywhere. I still had some money saved from my engineering job, but it wasn't going to last too much longer.

Out of partial desperation—and because I wanted to get going, and because I wanted to show my parents I was indeed employable as a journalist—I took a volunteer gig at Rogers TV in Mississauga. It was a great opportunity, and fortunately for me, my timing was perfect, because there was an opening for the host of *Peel Living*. It was a show featuring the best that the region—Mississauga, Brampton, and Caledon—has to offer. The job didn't pay, but I figured the experience wouldn't hurt, working alongside a producer and cameraman. Looking back now, I can see that getting my foot in the door there was so key. And for a lot of reasons.

Luckily, my parents were very preoccupied with building their house, a massive project that started in 2003 and was finalized two years later. Jeannie was all in on the details, and she led that project. She sat down with the architects and explained how she wanted the living room and dining room to look. How big the windows should be. My mum was an expert planner, and it brought her so much joy. She was a perfectionist, too, but not so regimented that she wasn't open to other ideas. People loved working with Mum because she was full of ideas and was also always open-minded.

"How's the design going?" I'd ask, and she'd light up with details about her dream kitchen with a giant island that we could all talk and gather and eat around. Kay, Nick, and I called her Martha Stewart because everything in our home always looked perfect, and she was now planning a new house with that same view. A home that would be perfect for our family.

When I was getting started in journalism, my parents were busy planning and building their house, and I was thankful for that. It was something else to talk about while I got my feet wet at work and figured things out for myself gradually. My parents didn't need to know all the ins and outs of my struggle to break into the industry. I was working on it!

With *Peel Living*, every week we would go to a new location in the region. I'd be in front of the camera to introduce our audience to a new restaurant in Brampton, or a garden opening in Caledon, or a honey festival in Mississauga. I was so green, and I wasn't very good, but they got what they paid for! Everything was a learning experience. For instance, we'd go to an old historical house in Brampton and I'd say something like "Look at this old house. It's been around since 1830. You can come on the weekend." Seriously. That was it. Nothing about the way I talked or looked was natural. I was stuck between being stiff as a board and overacting like a cheeseball, getting a little too excited about the new flowers blooming in the city's park.

I even changed the way I spoke, which I only noticed because my friends started pointing out to me that I was no longer using slang of any kind. Like, I didn't even say "didn't." I said "did not." I thought I should speak formally on television. When I really think about it, I realize I was attempting to be formal in every way.

I was uptight. Self-conscious. I was trying to be something that I thought the viewers and my bosses wanted. What I thought a host should be.

I'll never forget my on-camera hit, live from the new dollar store. The camera cut to me from the station with "We're going to Evanka Osmak, who's live at the dollar store!" And I said: "Oh my gosh, it's so fun here—there's parties, balloons, there's cake! There's a great deal on umbrellas, so come get an umbrella before they sell out!" It wasn't even raining.

The natural thing would've been to watch other reporters and emulate some of what I saw them do, but I never did. I wanted to find my own way. I didn't check to see what style of clothing I should be wearing. My on-TV education was being on TV, and my attitude was that that I'd figure it out. Mum would tune in every chance she got, and she was never critical, even though she had plenty to work with there. "You sounded great, Evanka," she'd tell me. "I'll have to check out that new dollar store."

I worked hard. I hustled. And I guess I did it in my own way. During my spare time—of which there was plenty—I tweaked my VHS résumé tape with my new material from *Peel Living*. I kept contacting stations. I reached out to editors around the area and see if I could rent their equipment so I could spruce up my audition tape, and I would add any new clips to it that I thought were strong.

Back then, it felt like it took forever to land an actual paying gig. That's probably because I hadn't been making money since May, and I was living at home and enjoying Jeannie's phenomenal cooking on a daily basis.

And then finally, in October, two months after I'd graduated, I got a call about an actual paying job. It was from a woman named Heather at Jack FM, in Orillia. No, it wasn't for television, but there was a radio host opportunity and she wanted to know: "Are you interested?" Orillia was about an hour and a half north of where my parents lived.

I needed to start making money. And with no other prospects, this seemed to me to be a great place to start. My salary: $10 an hour for thirty hours a week. This was a part-time job. Do the math, and you know I wasn't going on any Starbucks coffee runs.

"Evanka, you know you can always come home," Mum reminded me.

Yes, I knew that. And I'd need to from time to time. I had left behind my stable career in engineering and a job that paid $44,000 a year to make ten bucks an hour in a town where I knew absolutely no one.

But I was *so* excited. My foot was in the door. I had a second shot. And hey, maybe this time I'd actually even love my career.

Roller Coaster

I step on the ice and take a few strides.

Hey, wait a minute . . . this feels different. In a good way.

I take another couple of strides.

Wow! I feel . . . dare I say . . . not so shaky?

It's our sixth session of skills, and I'm lost in thought while I'm skating these first few warm-up laps. My inner monologue is full of the most pumped-up self-talk—"You're an all-star!"—even if I'm still the worst skater on the ice. I wonder if Coach Ethan has seen the improvement I'm feeling right now as I skate.

Then Coach Ethan's whistle blasts me out of my daydream.

The whistle means we have to stop and change directions. For me, that's a slow turn. I feel like a clunky robot. There's a rigidness in my body while I turn, slow motion. No, I still can't stop. It's baby steps here.

But as I turn, I'm smiling because I'm feeling that wee bit of swagger. A touch of confidence. Because that wobbly, super-uneasy Osmak of two and three weeks ago is now darn near steady! Ish. I feel pretty good on these blades. On this ice.

The last couple of weeks, it felt like my ankles were constantly at work, just trying to keep me upright. Was I an ankle burner? Definitely. But now I feel *almost* strong on my blades. I hope that I no longer look like a gust of wind could blow me over.

A woman named MJ has quickly become one of my favourite people to talk to at skills sessions every week. She's in her sixties or so, and has a daughter my age, who plays a lot of volleyball. MJ is average height, with white hair and a giant smile she always wears on the ice. I gravitated toward her a couple weeks ago as I walked into the dressing room, because she's so warm and has such a friendly face, and she's always talking to someone while we get ready to go on the ice. We've been chatting ever since. My first hockey friend! MJ's been playing for a couple of years now, and she's way better than I am. Okay, I know: Who isn't?

My point is, what a difference a few skates makes. I didn't start my hockey career as a good, decent, mediocre, or even somewhat-passable skater. I'm a total beginner. The finer hockey skills—using a stick, or handling and shooting and passing a puck—are all taking a back seat right now to my main aim, which is to learn how to move without falling and feeling and looking like a baby deer taking her first steps. And I think I'm getting there.

That I've made progress already feels amazing. I'm also turning left *way* better than I was a week ago. (Don't ask about turning right.) When I step onto the ice, I'm not pausing to make sure I don't fall and toss my gear everywhere. I step onto the ice and I glide, almost smoothly, with my stick out for balance. That's what the pros do, right? Definitely.

Okay, I'm not quite comfortable. Not yet. But I'm as comfortable as I've ever been in skates. And gosh, does that ever feel good. To make progress. The hour-long skills session goes by in what feels like fifteen minutes. MJ and I walk out to the parking lot together, bags slung over our shoulders, and she asks about the kids. She always does now—she knows all about Blake and George. "Blake just started taking swimming lessons—he's loving it," I tell her. MJ is pumped. "That's the best!" she says. Like me, MJ prefers kids when they're mobile, like her two grandkids now are. The baby stage? It's just not for me, or her.

As I say goodbye to MJ, we both yell, "Can't wait for next week!" while we toss our equipment in our cars, and I think of all this great progress happening in my family. Blakey Baby is swimming with a big smile on his face. George has been ripping around on his bike without training wheels. I'm taking strides on the ice without feeling wobbly.

But as soon as I get settled in my car, my mind goes back to my mum. Hockey has become one of the few places where I can distract myself from what Jeannie's going through. Honestly, I'm having too much fun on the ice to focus on anything but my hockey skills. But as soon as that's over, as I sit in the car and put the keys in the ignition, that awful reality hits: As much as I'm improving on the ice, my mum's health is deteriorating at lightning speed. We're going in two separate directions.

Absolutely everything makes me think of Jeannie these days. I go shopping: *Oh man, Jeannie would love this outfit.* I go for a walk on a sunny day: Jeannie would be talking about the flowers—she loved her garden. She's been devoted to maintaining and taking care of it, making sure her perennials were cut back to ensure optimum growth the next year, weeding nearly every other day in the summer to keep it looking pristine. Taking special care of her hydrangeas.

George is always asking me to march around the room and clap like we're in "Nama's marching band." It's a game they used to play together all the time. We walk around clapping and I love it, but I also can't help but think that Nama will never be able to be the leader of her band again. She can't walk with that kind of zip anymore. I think about how Blake will never get to experience Nama's band. How Blake will barely get to experience Nama, period. He'll never be picked up by Nama and zoomed around the room like an airplane. He'll never spend a weekend sleeping over at Nama's. Adam and I call her "a professional grandmother," because she is. Her face lights up around the kids. She has endless energy. At least, she did.

Jeannie is regressing. Shrinking. And while we've been watching it happen slowly for months, reality has hit harder since the diagnosis. I go to visit Jeannie for the first time since we found out she has ALS, and now that we know what's happening to Mum, it's like the disease is showing itself to us at warp speed. And now that we know the diagnosis, we can no longer deny that my mum is slipping away.

I know I need to be positive when I see Jeannie and Borden. I walk into my parents' house in Oakville, and they are both in the living room. Jeannie is sitting in her same spot on the muted green couch, underneath that same blanket—a miniature duvet, brown on one side, yellow on the other. Mum is always cold now.

"Hi!" I say with the biggest smile my face can muster. I'm super enthusiastic. It's the only thing I can do.

I give both of my parents a giant hug, starting with Jeannie. She feels so small, but I refuse to think about why, to fixate on how she's probably lost ten pounds since I saw her as many days ago. I hug Borden and he gives me a tight hug back, and an equally tight smile.

When Jeannie sees me, she's smiling, too. Thank goodness. I have no idea what she's thinking, but I wonder if she's in some sort of denial, or if her brain isn't fully able to understand her circumstances. I figure either we're both deciding we'll behave like nothing has changed, or maybe my mum doesn't feel like it has. I'm just happy she's smiling.

I plan to stay as positive and upbeat as possible for my whole visit. I immediately launch into anything exciting I can tell them. "Blakey is loving swimming and he's even doing cannonballs!" I say, and I pull out my phone to show the video evidence. "So cute," Jeannie says in her now-always-raspy voice. She clears her throat after she speaks, trying to get more air. "A little fish," she adds, smiling.

Jeannie's communication skills are basic and simple, but she's involved in conversation. Though it is mostly one-sided, and I'm doing the heavy lifting. I show her a picture of George playing hockey and she responds with "That's great."

Adam and I have just told the kids that Nama is "sick" at this point. We aren't going to explain everything to them—they wouldn't understand it, and knowing that she's dying would crush them, like it has crushed us. But what makes Jeannie smile the most is hearing about George and Blake. So I tell her everything.

"Blake started eating broccoli! George is learning to play the piano and I think by Christmas he'll have 'Rudolph the Red-Nosed Reindeer' nailed, and we can all sing along . . . George keeps telling me he wants a dog. No way, Georgie! Blakey probably throws more food than he eats. He's been saying 'Dorge' instead of 'George.' I love how much the boys love each other. We just signed George up for hockey, and he also loves swimming, and obviously he runs everywhere . . ." I go on and on and on and on.

I'll bring the kids the next time to see her, because I know there's nobody my mum would rather see than George and Blake. She's the best Nama out there. But selfishly, I want my time with her, and COVID is still everywhere. We don't want to get her sick. George is in school, where germs are rampant, and we want to keep her safe. We're all wearing masks, and there's a fear there. But also a feeling of "Screw this pandemic," because how much time do we have left with my mum?

A friend of mine recently lost her dad, and she barely saw him because he fell ill at home, and she was so scared of making him sick by visiting. They'd see each other outside, and she'd stand ten feet away. He was on oxygen, but she had no idea he was dying. When he passed away, she told me she wished she'd visited more, that it rips her apart that she didn't. Knowing this, that's how I decide we have to spend Jeannie's last days: with her, as carefully as possible.

I've now told close friends about my mum's diagnosis. Like Lara—I told her first. "I'm sorry," she said, and we both cried. And truly, there wasn't much to say: It was awful. Nadine, our makeup artist, now knows. Her dad died when she was nineteen, and she's been such a source of support. And Ken, who I told at the end of October of 2021. He and his wife have been incredibly kind, and when I see Ken at work, he gives me a little hug or pats my back. I know he cares and he's doing everything he can to support me.

I've started to tell more people because I'm so emotional. I can't keep it in, and it's so obvious that something is wrong. Anything sets me off and brings me to tears. When I told my friend and for-mer colleague, Arash Madani, his immediate reaction was "Oh shit." A friend of his had died of ALS and he knew how serious it was.

We don't know how much time we have left with my mum.

That's part of the reason that, for this visit, I'm here on my own. I want my full attention to be on her, instead of worrying about whether George and Blake are going to break some of my parents' lamps or draw on their sofas.

"Do you want to go for a little walk, Mum?" I ask. "It's sunny out today." I'm always trying to get Jeannie to move while she still can. But I have no idea how tired it makes her, or how she feels in terms of strength. Is she strong enough to go for a five-minute walk? None of us know how hard anything is for her because she doesn't tell us. She doesn't say much of anything lately.

She just shakes her head no. She doesn't want to go for a walk. "Can I get you something to eat?" I ask. Another no. "You have to eat," I tell her, but Jeannie isn't keen on food these days. "You need your strength, you can't lose so much weight," I say. She says she would like some tea instead. "I can get it," she adds.

Jeannie gets up to walk to the kitchen, which is about twenty steps from the couch she's been sitting on. Her pace is slow and deliberate. Seeing her move now, it's like my 72-year-old mum is suddenly 102 years old.

I join her and we make tea together. Then I flip through my phone and ask: "What do you think of this outfit?" I show her the dress I wore on Wednesday night at work, a blue number with white stripes. She smiles. "I like it," she says.

Ever since I started at Sportsnet, Jeannie has watched me religiously and has either texted or called after every show to tell me what she thought of what I was wearing that night, or if she thought I was particularly funny, or if she had a suggestion, usually about my style. "Great dress!" she'd text, along with a heart emoji, and maybe even a fire one. "Loved when you made fun of Ken's tie!" she'd write.

Or "Maybe you should wear your hair up tomorrow," she'd say, and my hair would be up the next night. I loved all her comments. My mum has great style, and a great sense of humour, too.

But those messages and calls stopped months ago. It was one of my first clues that something was wrong with my mum. She had stopped watching. Stopped reacting. One night I wore big hoop earrings, and they got a solid reaction from her the last time. She loved them, so I wondered if she'd write to tell me she was glad they were back. But the second time I wore them, I got no reaction from her. It seems like a small thing, but Jeannie watched me the way some people don't miss an episode of *Jeopardy!* I was her must-see TV. And I loved being her must-see TV. And now, suddenly, everything has changed.

We slowly make our way back to the living room, tea in hand. Borden had said hi when I arrived, but not long after that, he went upstairs to his office. Tato spends lots of time up there these days when Nick or Kay or I visit. My dad has a big, rolltop wooden antique desk with all his files. He'll sit there and do paperwork and look at his computer. He's not consulting anymore, but he's helping out Nick, who buys land and develops it, and manages properties.

It's avoidance, probably. Needing breaks, definitely. I don't think Tato knows what to do, what to say. It's hard for him to watch the love of his life dying, regressing every day.

As worried as I am about Jeannie, I worry about Tato, too. I don't think he understands how grave this disease is. How quickly it's progressing. And how much is out of my mum's control. Which is everything.

And because he's so close to my mum and is with her basically every minute, maybe to Borden, ALS isn't progressing at lightning speed. But I think Tato is in denial.

I think he believes if we get food into her, and if she puts on some weight and can be a little active, then she'll be okay. He's constantly sending us articles about the disease. Just yesterday he sent one to us kids that detailed reasons for living with ALS, and so many of those reasons were family. To be around family, to spend time with family, to live out your final days surrounded by loved ones.

Even though he's reading these articles and sending them to us, part of Borden, I think, still believes she can be okay enough to live with this. But it's so clear to me that this is an impossible dream. Jeannie is going downhill fast, and there's no turning back or slowing down.

Last week, she was able to eat things like cut-up pears and bananas. Now, suddenly, everything needs to be pureed. It's all soups and smoothies that Tato has been preparing for her.

This is another thing I notice at my parents' house: the sudden role reversal that's been happening, starting a few months ago. Their entire lives together, Borden has been taken care of by Jeannie. She cleaned. Washed and folded their clothes. Paid their bills. Shopped for groceries. Made and planned their meals. Organized their social calendar. Planned trips—a big one every year, like Australia, or a safari in Africa, or a river cruise on the Danube.

And soon, Tato will be on his own. Is he going to plan to meet up with his friends? Is he going to go on trips alone? Will he make himself healthy meals? These thoughts make me want to curl up into a ball and cry.

While Jeannie's still with us, Borden is being forced into these new roles. My mum can't cook, and she can hardly lift a fork with food on it to feed herself. She's starting to have trouble swallowing, too. Suddenly my dad is making her those soups and shakes so she gets her nutrients, and trying to get food into her, as well as trying to cook for himself. He's bearing all of this, and truthfully, it's all too much, because he's watching the woman he's loved for more than fifty years wither away at the same time. They had just celebrated their fiftieth wedding anniversary in August of 2021.

I think Tato's feeling pressure, too. Since he's the caretaker, he doesn't want to do anything wrong. His face looks tight and gaunt. His smiles are forced. It's so clear to me that this isn't the happy household it used to be. When I walked through that door, and if my parents were on that green couch, both of them would fly up off it and give me a big hug. Neither Borden nor Jeannie has the energy now, and Jeannie also doesn't have the mobility anymore to lift both arms up for a good squeeze. Blake, who's one and a half, will never know the Nama who chases after him and picks him up and plays with him and tickles him.

But I can't think about any of this right now. I can't fixate on it. So it's back to pictures and videos.

"Look, Mum!" I say, hitting play on a video of George, who's mainlining cake. "You know Georgie—he loves his desserts."

"I love all my grandkids so much," Jeannie says, and her green-grey eyes turn toward the carpet. They look sad and dull. I can see in her tired little eyes and hear in her weak voice that she knows she's not getting better. That she doesn't have much time left to be with or see her grandkids. Or her kids. Or anyone. That this is not something she'll recover from.

But it's back to little smiles from me as we focus on happy things only. Because honestly: What else are we supposed to do?

Just a few months ago, Adam, George, Blake, and I moved out of our house and into a rental home nearby, while we do a full renovation on our home. It's been delayed because of COVID, but finally it's underway. This renovation and planning of our new home is something my mum was so invested in when we started talking about it two years ago.

She'd spend actual hours a night going over drawings. She was my sounding board for any interior-decorating ideas, and it was a creative outlet for her, too. Jeannie would earmark articles from *House & Home* magazine featuring a kitchen she loved, or she'd put a Post-it that said *Check this out!* on a photo of what she thought was the perfect shade of brown for hardwood floors. I swear she gave me ten folders of articles and pictures to review for inspiration. The woman was a walking, talking Pinterest board of interior design. "Evanka, isn't this just beautiful?" she'd say, lighting up, grinning ear to ear as she pointed to a modern-looking kitchen with a giant fridge and plenty of sunlight, thanks to that window above the sink.

Today, as I'm scrolling through my phone looking for pictures and videos I think will make her happy, I show Mum a photo of the bathroom tiles Adam and I are considering for the main floor. We're torn between a muted stone colour and simple design, or an all-white clean look. My mum shows no reaction. It breaks my heart because Jeannie *loves* this stuff. Devours it. Two years ago, my mum would've seen those two pictures and talked for an hour about the merits of each tile, and her eyes would've lit up when she saw her favourites. Then she would've FaceTimed me to give me more of her thoughts. And clipped seven articles featuring tiles she liked better.

Today, she just looks at the photos of the tiles without saying anything. So I head straight back to pictures of the grandkids and scroll to a video that George made just for her.

"Nama—watch this!" George says as he races around our backyard, doing cartwheels and firing pucks on a net we have set up. George ends off his show with a quick wave and: "I love you, Nama!"

"I love you, too, George," my mum says quietly, looking at my phone. "George, I love you so, so much."

My heart swells and breaks at the same time.

Welcome to the Desert

I began my first-ever paying journalism gig in November of 2004, as Jack FM's evening news correspondent in Orillia. I'd deliver two-minute updates every weekday from three to six p.m. I took it as seriously as Barbara Walters did, too.

I'd been told I have a gravelly voice that's good for the radio or TV, and I leaned into it in Orillia. I talked like a journalism robot. "City council is voting on a new parking bylaw," I'd say, even-toned, like it was the Most Important News on Earth. "A new coffee shop is opening downtown."

Every weekday, I'd provide short updates on what was going on in Orillia and surrounding towns like Barrie and Port Severn. I'd go to hospital functions. Store openings. On Monday nights, I'd suffer through city council meetings (Mondays were not my favourites). I'd gather the important information on things like crosswalks and noise levels and cattle crossings. I'm not joking: Sometimes those cows got in the way of traffic.

"That happened in Gilbert Plains sometimes, too," Mum told me. She knew all too well about the traffic the cows could cause, having grown up in a farming community. And now her daughter was reporting on them. She must've felt so proud!

Jack FM was a start, but this wasn't my dream gig, by any stretch. And though I was on the airwaves, I was certainly not living the dream in Orillia. I stayed in the city only when I needed to: I lived in a Holiday Inn Monday through Thursday, then I'd drive home to Oakville after my Friday shift.

Mum would always grab my laundry at the front door and take care of it before I even had the chance to do it myself. She'd cook some of my favourite meals, like fall-off-the-bone ribs. My parents were now part-time empty nesters—outside of weekends—and I know they both enjoyed having me back home.

But mostly I lived in a hotel. There were hardly any other guests, so it meant housecleaning almost every day because the staff didn't have much else to do. It also meant I was eating out every night at Swiss Chalet. It was the same order every time—chicken wrap, hold the tomato and mayo, please. That Christmas, all I asked for were Swiss Chalet gift cards, and did they ever come in handy.

But when I say I was very serious about my job, I'm very serious about that. One day I went to an elementary school and attended a 911 demonstration. As the police were going through what to do in the event of an emergency, I literally had my own.

It was really hot in the gym, and I hadn't drunk much water that day. I felt pretty weak, but I couldn't have anticipated what happened next. As the police officers were talking to the kids, boom: I fell to the gym floor—I actually fainted. I swear I wasn't part of the demonstration! But in retrospect, I couldn't have chosen a better place to have a minor medical emergency. I was the perfect model—except the teachers hurried the kids out of the room so the

EMS could help me. I'm told that when I woke up, I was speaking gibberish, maybe Ukrainian. I know hardly any Ukrainian, except for swear words, which my baba in Manitoba taught me. My parents know Ukrainian, and they'd speak it to each other when we were kids so we didn't understand what they were saying. My mum would often smile at us as she talked to Dad in a language we didn't know. So sneaky. (I realize now how amazing it is to have a secret language in front of your kids, since George is now old enough to read, and Adam and I can't spell out words. Like I-C-E C-R-E-A-M if we're planning to have Häagen-Dazs after the kids go to bed.)

It's funny looking back on that moment, but of course I didn't talk about it on the radio the next day. Because I was a Serious News Reporter, not somebody who faints and then makes fun of herself on air. I do regret that now, because the deejay I worked with was trying so hard to make me less of a robot when we talked on air. He would've loved that story!

The deejay's name was Tom Shock—I can't remember if that was his real name or if he made it up, but it's perfect. And Tom Shock would be back at the station and he'd throw to me—introduce me—on air if I was about to tee up the traffic report, or I was reporting from a local event. "Evanka, what's happening? How's the java at the new coffee shop?" he'd ask. And then I'd give him . . . nothing. "Today in downtown Orillia marks the opening of a new coffee shop, and blah, blah, blah." Poor Tom Shock! I was a serious young lady reporting Super Important News. I couldn't have fun. This was my job.

But Tom Shock wouldn't give up, probably because he was trying to fill time on air. "What's the best concert you'd ever been to?" he'd ask as he was throwing to me for a news update that he knew included an upcoming concert in Barrie. And after about a month or so on the job, I finally started to give Tom Shock something to work with. "Definitely Backstreet Boys," I told him. "Brian was my favourite. So dreamy!" With Tom Shock's help, I started to realize I could talk more off script, that I didn't have to take myself so seriously. Tom Shock was the first person to show me you can be yourself on air. That having a personality can help bring in listeners and keep them engaged.

I learned that important lesson at Jack FM, and I started to take it with me to other jobs. It served me well as I started to work toward getting paid to be on TV. While I was at Jack FM, I was still volunteering for Rogers TV back in Mississauga on weekends, co-hosting *Peel Living*. I was commuting home every weekend, and it was the highlight of my week. There was still no doubt in my mind that I wanted to be on TV.

In those days, I wished I felt more relaxed and able to talk to anybody about anything, like my mum could. I think we could've thrown her on air and she would've been immediately relaxed and likeable. I don't know exactly what it was about her, but people really liked my mum even after meeting her just briefly. She would walk into a brand-new social situation and make an impression. She sought out a connection with everyone she came across, and seemed to always fit right in. It was one of Mum's best qualities: She could get along with anyone, and talk about any topic comfortably.

And here her daughter was, robotic, and failing to connect with listeners and viewers because I was just so stiff.

That was just part of the issue with my job situation, truly. I knew I couldn't keep going like that forever. The experience was good, and hopefully I'd learn to be less of a robot on air, but living out of a hotel was expensive, and since I was only working six hours a day at $10 an hour, it wasn't exactly paying the bills. Thankfully I had savings left over. But I was definitely drinking a lot of free Holiday Inn coffee.

Every week, I sent half a dozen of my carefully bubble-wrapped VHS tape demos to television stations. The tape featured me reporting news that happened at Seneca College, and my newer stuff from *Peel Living* as I got more experience there.

I was applying to every job in TV, in cities and towns I'd never heard of. I'd talked to a guy I knew from high school who worked at one of the Score TV stations, in Toronto, and he told me only to accept jobs in sports. So that's what I applied for at first, but then I got so desperate that I was applying to news jobs, weather jobs, you name it. I wanted to get my foot in the door. And I applied mostly in the States. Honestly, I thought that between living somewhere in rural Canada versus somewhere south, I'd take the latter. It had everything to do with the sun. And my American passport meant a station didn't have to secure a work visa for me.

I probably sent out one hundred tapes all over the US, no exaggeration. I scoured job websites daily. I was taking my shot and shooting everywhere. What I didn't understand at the time was the market system, and that it was highly unlikely a station in Dallas or any city with a top ten news station would hire a rookie like me. But I sent my tape to them anyway. I sent my tape to any station with an address.

Self-doubt started to creep in after I didn't hear back from anyone for months. *Maybe I'm not that good*, I thought. *Why had I made such a wild career change?*

And then, in February, after three months of living in Orillia,

I got a job offer from a station called KYMA in a place called . . . Yuma. The email from the news director popped into my inbox. Was it spam? Where was Yuma? Was it even a real place? What station was this? I didn't even remember applying there.

I entered "Yuma" into Google immediately. It turned out to be in Arizona—sweet! I thought I'd really enjoy the desert. Okay, except for the snakes. *There better not be any snakes.* Even seeing them on TV makes me hysterical. I run out of the room.

The offer was to host a morning show, the pay was $19,000 (USD!) a year, and I'd be living on the USA-Mexico border. I'd never been to Arizona before. I knew nothing about immigration issues. And the snakes: No, thank you.

But I knew right away that this was my dream job as a rookie TV anchor.

I called my parents and laid out the details, and to my absolute shock, Borden and Jeannie actually supported my decision. Tato said: "You've got to take it."

"That sounds like a wonderful opportunity, Evanka," Mum said.

I knew it, and I was going to take the job anyway, but I really didn't expect that from Mum and Tato. Looking back, I wonder if they thought this job would be so bad that it would make me want to return to my steady old engineering job.

I wonder if Jeannie said: "She'll see a snake and she'll want to come home!" And then my parents laughed together about my path back to engineering.

Or maybe it's because they believed in me, and they saw how seriously I was taking myself and this new career path. I was doing it without their help. I was doing it on my own. And how can you stand in the way of someone who's trying to figure out where they belong? Jeannie had done the exact same thing at sixteen when she moved across the country on her own, so surely she could understand.

I felt like I now had my parents' full support to continue to pursue journalism. I think they both trusted me to figure it out for myself.

I was ready to go to Yuma. It wasn't a sports job, but it was a foot in the door. I called the news director to accept the job and he interrupted me and said: "Before you get too excited, let me go over again what your role would be and what your pay is."

I told him none of that mattered. I needed to start somewhere, and there was no way I was turning that job down. So I was moving to . . . the Lettuce Capital of America. No joke. That's Yuma.

"Hey, Tato, are you up for a road trip in the good ol' family station wagon?" I asked my dad. "It could be fun to head to the desert! We'll eat lots of lettuce once we get to Yuma!"

And you know what? My dad was ready to road trip. "You bet!" he said.

He was going to support his daughter's cockamamie dream after all. But he made sure to remind me: "If this doesn't work out, you can always go back to engineering."

Emotional Baggage

hopped into the back seat of my parents' SUV. Dad was driving and Mum, who got in with Tato's help, was sitting shotgun. He'd clicked her seat belt shut, since she didn't have the strength to do that herself.

It was October 6, 2021, and we were going shopping at the Sherway Gardens mall, in the west end of Toronto. Well, at least Jeannie and I were shopping. Tato decided he'd drop us off and wait in the car.

This trip was my idea, because I'd been noticing a lot of changes to my mum's appearance over the previous couple of months. Her clothes were hanging off her—literally, hanging. She'd probably lost twenty pounds in the past four weeks. It didn't matter that she ate creamy soups and drank Boost shakes to up her calorie intake. Nothing stuck to her. Every time I'd visit, she'd be wearing the same black sweatpants and navy sweater. And often her clothes had bits of food stuck to them.

It was like Jeannie didn't notice or didn't care about how she looked, and it was jarring to see her this way. Because for forty years, the entire time I'd known her, my mum had been polished. She always cared how she looked. She rarely even had a strand of hair out of place. But suddenly she was unkempt, not at the standard she'd held for herself for all of her life.

I figured it still must matter to her, because I knew it always had. But the last thing I wanted to do was embarrass my mum. I also understood that Jeannie felt most comfortable now in sweatpants and a sweatshirt.

I considered all of this, and so I asked her, "Should we go shopping and pick out a few new outfits for you?"

I was so happy to hear Jeannie say, in her now-croaky voice: "That would be really nice."

It made my week to know Jeannie still had that love of shopping. My mum and I have been on countless shopping trips together. Mum was the one orchestrating cross-border journeys to Buffalo, New York, when we kids were young. That was back when the Gap wasn't even in Canada.

Nick, Kay, Jeannie, and I would all pile into the car, wearing our oldest clothes with holes in them, and we'd hit up Walden Galleria. With so many discounts, that mall is like a candy store for Canadians, especially when our dollar is strong. Do you need new Nike sneakers? Why not buy two pairs at this price?

Once we'd all bought a bunch of new stuff, we'd head to the bathroom and throw out all the old clothes we were wearing, and we'd put the new ones on, layer upon layer upon layer, making sure we ripped off all the price tags. I swear Jeannie once had on six layers of shirts and three layers of pants and shiny new shoes when we drove through customs.

"Anything to declare?" the agent would ask. "No," Jeannie would answer, smiling. And then off we'd drive, cheering when we made it through.

Often, Kay and Nick would decide the trip wasn't worth it—they didn't care about fashion the way Jeannie and I did. So it was usually just Jeannie and me on those cross-border sprees. And oh, was Jeannie ever a great shopper. She was so good at finding cool necklaces and beautiful shoes. As she got older, she knew which designers she liked. Max Mara. She had endless pairs of Salvatore Ferragamo shoes. And countless pairs of black pants. A conservative black outfit was basically her uniform. She always looked smart and timeless. When I was younger, I remember thinking her style was boring. But the more I age, the more I realize having an identity in style and clothing makes things less complicated. I just curse that my mum wore size 9 and, with my size 11 boats, I could never borrow her sweet heels.

Black pants and a nice long-sleeved blouse with a sharp blazer overtop was my mum's go-to look. It was always long sleeves for Jeannie, too, because she hated the way her arms looked. I didn't get why she was self-conscious about her arms, and I never asked her why, but she wanted to cover them. She'd wear long-sleeved, flowy shirts in the summer, with a fabulous, big-brimmed hat.

We'd always get together and go to Blue Jays games as a family, after all us kids moved out. I'd show up in jeans and a T-shirt, and my mum would pull up in a giant hat, a beautiful, flowing white blouse, and some nice navy-blue pants and sandals. So we'd razz her, obviously. "Mum, can't you just wear a T-shirt and a baseball cap?" I'd ask, laughing. Jeannie would laugh right back. But hey, she looked great. This isn't to say my mum never dressed down—she did. She wore her sweats, for sure. But even then, she looked polished. It helped that she always had nicely blow-dried hair and minimalist makeup on her face. She almost always had a set of pearls in her ears, too. Jeannie loved her pearls.

I hadn't seen my mum in those pearl earrings in the months leading up to our shopping trip. Or wearing makeup. Jeannie wore the same black sweatpants she had on the last time I visited, and the same dark crewneck sweatshirt. The pants and shirt were both too big for her.

I figured we should add a few new items to that uniform, some sweats that would fit her better. I also knew that taking Jeannie shopping would be a nice break for Tato, and I wanted him to have a bit of time to himself. As mentioned, Borden decided he'd drop us off at the mall and wait until we were done shopping. "We won't be longer than an hour, Tato," I told him. I knew that any longer than that and my mum would be tired. This would be our shortest shopping trip ever, but we'd make the best of it. We had to.

Tato pulled up right in front of Nordstrom. I decided to take her there because it's a great store with lots of options, and one of Jeannie's favourite spots. It's convenient, too: It has an escalator and it isn't hidden in the mall somewhere. You can access it from outside, right from the parking lot.

Borden helped Jeannie get her mask on, while I put on mine—this was still at the height of COVID, and we couldn't risk getting my mum sick. Because her breathing wasn't coming easy, I knew we had to be quick in there, since wearing a mask made accessing air even harder than it already was for her. One of the symptoms of ALS is weakening chest muscles, which makes breathing difficult. It's why respiratory problems are one of the leading causes of death among people with ALS. But I wasn't thinking about that as I got out of the car in front of Nordstrom and took my mum's hand. Nope. Happy thoughts only. We were going shopping.

I walked slowly with her through the front doors of the store. The women's section is upstairs, so we made our way to the escalator. I held my mum's hand as we both got on, and I kept my arm around her tiny waist as we headed upstairs. I held her steady as we stepped off, too.

Jeannie used to browse through racks and look at outfits and pull things out and say, "What do you think of this?" But this shopping experience was different. It was me asking her: "How about this?" Her look was almost vacant. She smiled from time to time, which I could tell even though she had a mask on, because I could see it in her eyes. I was making sure to smile the whole time. I knew I needed to be happy and light around Mum. This had to be fun, like all our previous shopping trips together.

I was trying to find something bright for her to wear. Jeannie looked pale and sallow, and she didn't wear makeup to try to brighten herself up. I found a fuchsia mock-neck turtleneck. "Nice and bright! What do you think, Mum?" Jeannie nodded yes. Bingo! I pulled out some jeans and she said: "I don't need those."

She still had an opinion on her clothes, which I loved. But I also wondered: Does she think she won't need jeans because she's dying? I needed to get that thought out of my head, and I kept the jeans draped over my arm. Then I yanked some bright blue sweatpants off the rack. "How about these?" Jeannie smiled and shook her head no. "Not my style."

I pulled out some black pants next. "You always look great in black," I said. I also grabbed a grey sweatsuit with pink hearts on it, a super-cozy outfit by P.J. Salvage. They make great leisure wear.

I wondered if I should get the matching set for myself, Kay, and my sister-in-law, Amy. Jeannie nodded at that heart sweatsuit and reached out to touch the soft fabric, and smiled. Perfect.

I had six items draped over my arm as we headed to the dressing room. I took a deep breath as we walked in. I was trying to act as normal as possible, but I knew I was about to do something I never expected to do: I had to change my mum into her clothes because she couldn't manage it herself. Jeannie had no strength in her hands to pull her pants up or down. To get a sweater over her head.

When I spotted the extra-big dressing room, I immediately walked in with her. I reminded myself I'd dressed George and Blake hundreds of times. That when they run around like wild animals while I try to dress them some days makes it way harder than this. Dressing Jeannie would be a piece of cake.

"Isn't this pretty?" I told her, holding up that fuchsia sweater again. Jeannie smiled and nodded. I helped her pull up her sweatshirt, slowly and deliberately. I held up her arms as I slowly pulled off the sweater, and then yanked it over her head. George always screams when I do that because he has a big head and it seems like kids' clothes have such small head holes. Jeannie didn't stir up any fuss.

I was doing my best to act like this wasn't a big deal at all, just a daughter getting her mum dressed. Just a couple of gals out for a shop. I pulled that bright fuchsia sweater over her head and Jeannie looked at herself in the mirror and smiled. "Mum, you look so good!" I told her. "We have to get it!"

"I love it," Jeannie said, still smiling.

We didn't even try on the heart-covered sweatsuit—we could

both tell it was a winner. There are no-look passes on the ice, and this was a no-try buy in the store. Jeannie took my advice on a pair of jeans with an elastic waist. "They'll be as comfy as sweats!" I assured her. She agreed, probably just to make me happy. And probably because she wanted to get out of there. She was pawing at her mask and clearing her throat. Having a lot of trouble breathing.

As we checked out, I talked to the cashier, put a big smile on, and was as social as possible. "Thanks so much," I told her. "My mum and I found some great stuff today."

In the back of my mind, I was wondering: *Will this be one of Jeannie's last social outings?* My mum, the social butterfly, rarely has her friends over anymore. How many more times will people get to see my mum? How many more times will she be out and about in public? But I had to turn that part of my brain off. So I kept my smile big, pulled out my phone, and took a selfie of Mum and me, both grinning behind our masks, right at the counter. I held up the big paper Nordstrom bag, and we looked as happy as a masked-up mom and daughter can be on their shopping spree.

I texted Borden once we were done, and by the time we reached the front of the store he was waiting for us. Mum immediately pawed at her mask as we hit the fresh air, and I pulled it off her. She let out a congested cough and loudly cleared her throat. We were in there about forty minutes, and I think that was more than enough for Jeannie.

"How did you make out?" Tato asked as he got out of the car so he could help Jeannie get in.

"Great!" I answered, and I told him everything we picked out. "She'll look great in that sweater," Tato said when he saw the fuchsia number. He was right, too. My dad isn't a shopper, but he knows what'll look great on the woman he's loved for more than half a century.

We drove back to my parents' place, where I'd left my car. As we said goodbye, I gave my mum a big hug. "I love you so much," I told her. "Thanks for coming shopping with me today."

"Thank you, Evanks," my mum said, giving me a weak hug back. It was everything I could do to keep the tears from falling. "I had a really nice time," she said.

I felt so thankful my mum could still have a nice time. I felt so thankful I could *take* my mum somewhere for a nice time.

Then I hugged Tato goodbye. "That meant a lot to your mum, Evanka," he said. "Thank you."

"Tato, she's so lucky to have you," I told him.

On the way home, I called Adam and started crying. "I had to get my mum dressed!" I said. "It's not fair! Why is this happening to her?"

"Oh, Evanks," Adam said. "I'm so sorry. But I know she appreciated that so much."

He was right, and I know she did. But I felt so sad.

I called Lara next, and I cried even harder with her. She lives in LA now with her three daughters and her husband. I told her all about the shopping trip. Lara knew exactly what to say.

"Evanka, make sure you get a picture of Jeannie in that turtleneck," she said. "I bet she looks amazing. I love that you two went shopping together."

I felt so, so thankful to have girlfriends like Lara to lean on. Shared experiences or not, there's nothing like calling up a friend and telling her what you're going through and knowing she's going to support you in exactly the way you need.

We talked the rest of my way home, about anything and every-thing. "Thank you, Lara," I said as I pulled into my driveway and said goodbye.

I headed out to visit my parents a couple of days after our shop-ping trip and brought them coffee. Jeannie was sitting in her spot on that muted green couch, wearing that grey sweatsuit with the hearts. The one we bought together.

She pointed at her outfit and smiled when she saw me. I smiled, too. And just like that, my day was made. So much about my mum had changed, but her love of shopping and a good outfit hadn't. Small glimmers of Jeannie were still there, and I was hanging on to them for dear life.

She looked spectacular in that new sweatsuit, too. But consid-ering how fast she was losing weight, how quickly she was dete-riorating, I wondered: How many more times would she even get to wear it?

Curveball

The drive to the desert to my first paying on-TV job was not your usual Osmak Family Road Trip.

First of all, it was just Borden and me. He loves road trips and I welcomed his support, but we'd never really spent that much time alone together—and this was a thirty-six-hour drive, just the two of us. I was a little unsure about how this was going to play out. What would we talk about for a day and a half, in a car together?

But any worries I had about dead air and awkward moments immediately evaporated. Tato was a great conversationalist—something I'd never realized as a child.

Once we arrived, my dad helped me get settled. We stayed in a hotel for a couple days while we looked for an apartment for me, and we found a nice one-bedroom close to the TV station. It reminded me of the apartment complex on *Melrose Place*. Except the apartment complex we found in Yuma was bigger, not as fancy, and worst of all, there weren't nearly as many hunky Hollywood actors as there were on the TV show. Sigh.

We decided it would do. We bought some basic furniture from Target, and we stocked the fridge with cheese and yogurt and eggs.

We got pasta and soups and chocolate-covered almonds for the cupboards.

A couple days later, Tato left. I was by myself in the Southwest. I felt like I was set up in my new home, and I was so excited. This wasn't the first time I'd lived on my own, but it was the first time I'd done so and hadn't been within a couple of hours of my parents. I felt like an adult. A professional.

Still, I was in touch with my mum daily. She was sure to call me if I hadn't called her yet, just to check in: "How's the desert?" she'd ask. "I haven't seen any snakes yet!" I'd tell her. Most of our conversations were in the early afternoon for me, since I was working early mornings.

I worked on the KYMA morning show, which was a combination of news and entertainment. It meant waking up at two a.m. so I could get to the station by two thirty. My co-anchors and I were on the air from five thirty until seven, and then we'd do updates every half hour until ten, before another show at noon for thirty minutes. It wasn't the easiest schedule, but since I had no kids or family, I figured it was the perfect time to be working those types of hours. And I had the energy to do it.

As I discovered, the station wasn't in the safest part of town. Although, at that hour, I'm not sure there were many safe parts in Yuma. Borden and I had checked it out before he left, and it had seemed fine. But it made me nervous to head into work at two thirty in the morning, in the dark, because I'm naturally a scaredy cat. I always have my head on a swivel, and I've been that way my whole life. It was all industrial and commercial buildings around the station, and at that hour, nothing was open. And since the station was so easily identifiable with its large sign, I always thought: *What if someone has a problem with the station? They could easily track us down.* Like I said: That's the way I operate. High alert.

I was often the first one there, and I'd have to enter a code on a keypad to get into the parking lot. But sometimes the gate to the parking lot wouldn't even be locked. So I'd take a deep breath and make my way in, and usually I'd be the only person in there for at least fifteen minutes, sometimes half an hour. I always heard sounds. I never felt settled until someone else showed up. But once my colleagues arrived, the place was an absolute hub of activity.

Every morning, the first thing I'd do when I got to work was email my mum. "I want to make sure you're safe!" she'd told me. Jeannie woke up at five thirty every morning to wait for me to let her know I was okay. Because of the time difference, my email would come in right around then: *Mum, I made it. Safe and sound. Xoxo E.* Her reply would be there a minute later: *Thank you. Love you! Talk soon!*

Most of the people at the station were around my age. About a third of us worked the morning show, and then the afternoon crew would take over, and then the evening staff. We were like ships passing in the night. And we were all young adults hoping this was a stepping stone to bigger things. I learned that KYMA was a 199 network in terms of rankings—if you're at a big one, you're top ten. We were nearly two hundredth. But we were there to learn, and none of us were making big money. My $19,000 salary (did I mention it was USD? Big cash, baby!) covered basic bills only, with a little left over after that. But this was a place to hone your craft, get good, and then move on to a bigger market.

My co-anchors were Alexis and Edgar, and we connected instantly. "EEEvanka?" Edgar asked when we first met. "Nailed it,

Edgar!" I replied. He was about five foot two and stockily built, and the guy was a legend around Yuma. If you were out in the field with a camera, people would ask: "Where's Edgar?" He'd be the guy wearing a giant hat with fruit on top, running around with a skirt on and a tube top at a parade, yelling things like: "This is the lettuce capital of America!" Everyone in town loved Edgar.

Alexis was a year younger than me, and the girl was *polished*. She'd been there for six months when I arrived, and you could see it, plain as day: Alexis had that "it" factor. She was glitzy and glamourous. She had that classic blond anchor hair, teased and hair-sprayed in the right places, and she wore dresses that flattered her. And then there was me, in the boxy blazers and with the boring straight hair. I dressed exactly as I had when I was an engineer. I didn't want to stand out. Compared to Alexis, I felt like I faded into the wall.

The three of us together was just comical. Like a parody of a morning show. Bright, shiny Alexis from California. Hilarious, joker Edgar from Salt Lake City, Utah. Robotic, plain Evanka from Canada.

Figuring out how to *be* on TV—how to stand, how to speak, how to move my arms—did not come naturally. I don't think *Peel Living* really prepared me for this, though I don't place any blame on that show. It was an amazing experience. The fact is, I hadn't gone out of my way to study for this. I had exactly zero confidence. I felt like I was trying to be someone else. Like I was putting on an act, some woman in her twenties playing the role of a Serious News Reporter. The best way I can describe it is, think of a time you've been very aware of all your movements. Even your breathing. That's how I felt in those early days in front of a camera. Like a bad actor.

"The high today in Yuma is one hundred and twenty degrees," I'd say, straight-faced. Serious.

I approached my job like I didn't want to stand out. Yes, I bought a bright pink blazer—I'd learned to wear bright colours on TV, to pop—but I wasn't over the top with my makeup or hair. I was very conservative. Hair straight and down. No eyeliner. Fake lashes? No way. Blue eye shadow? Leave that to Alexis, who could pull it off.

This was well before the days of YouTube how-to makeup videos, which really would've helped me. So instead, I winged it. I ordered everything from M.A.C cosmetics, and I thought: *This'll work. I'll spread this foundation all over my face. This should shine nice and bright on TV.*

Our nighttime news anchor, Nineveh, wore blue eye shadow, almost all the way up to her forehead. She just owned it, and it looked good. But nobody at KYMA told us how to prepare ourselves to look good on TV. We made it up as we went. Wardrobe? Winged that, too. A vertical-striped black-and-white suit? Sure, I'd give that a whirl, as long as it wasn't too flashy.

Everything was new to me, but my biggest learning curve was the stories and the fact we were actually covering news as it happened. There were really big stories that came our way, and because we were a border town, we always covered issues pertaining to illegal immigration, and the town had a very strong military presence. That was all so unfamiliar to me, and among the nearly daily goings-on that we'd feature on the broadcast. The variety I got at the station was incredible.

One of my first lessons was in weather. You couldn't say it was hot in Yuma unless it was at least 110 degrees. Yuma is known as the sunniest place on earth for a reason. "Evanka, if you say one hundred is hot, locals will be upset. They'll know you're not from here," Alexis explained. "Just say it's warm." That was my first lesson, learned the hard way, after calling ninety-nine degrees "hot." (I maintain, to this day, that ninety-nine is hot.)

I also had to master Spanish names, as a Canadian who'd never taken Spanish and had little exposure to it thus far in my life. I'd mispronounce a name like Luis Villa, saying the *l*'s like you would in English. Another learning curve for me, which Edgar and Alexis helped me out with. (That's something that would be a big problem for me later in my career. We'll get into that later. It was not good!)

Only three weeks into my time there, a Harrier jet crashed into a local house, and, since it was a military jet, we were never told the reason it went down. It was all pretty hush-hush and mysterious— the military kept things under wraps. But in addition to crashing into that house, its remains were spread across the backyards of four different houses. The jet was in pieces. It was all anyone in Yuma was talking about. Thankfully, nobody was hurt, because nobody had been home when it happened, but it gave us plenty of national and local attention. And that was a massive eye-opener for me. Everyone at the station sprung into action. They knew what they were doing.

Me? I was just wondering how the heck I could help. I felt so green, thinking I had to get up to speed quickly, like I wasn't prepared for this. I didn't know how to be live on a big scene. I didn't really know how to report. I had to learn on the job. We'd be doing our show and we'd throw live to a reporter on the scene: "What's going on out there, Rita?" I'd ask. I felt like I didn't know the right questions to ask, how to get more information. Then Alexis would chime in with a much better follow-up, like, "Rita, what are you hearing from people in the neighbourhood about how they saw this jet come down?" That drew out a great answer.

I remember feeling vulnerable that day. Ill prepared. Not very good at my job. With six months under her belt, Alexis knew exactly what she was doing, while I was her rookie sidekick.

Work was stressful, but Yuma did manage to start to feel like home pretty early on. Mum visited a couple of weeks in, and she helped make it feel that way. She did my laundry and took me to Costco so I could stock up on items like granola bars and oranges. She bought me more makeup at M.A.C, because I needed to smear it all over my face. We went to Home Depot to buy plants. "It'll make you feel more at home," Mum swore. As we were leaving the store, it was about 120 degrees outside and I looked at my mum's face and she was literally pouring with sweat.

"Are you okay, Mum?" I asked. "Your face is dripping like an ice cream cone!"

Mum nearly dropped the plant she was holding, she was laughing so hard. And then on any future visits to the desert she'd ask: "How's my face? Do I look like an ice cream cone?" and we'd laugh all over again.

The first Christmas I spent in Yuma, I didn't get much time off, since I was so junior at our office. So Mum planned our family Christmas in San Diego to be closer to me. "I want the whole family together," Mum said, and she made it happen. Since everyone else had the time off, she figured they could all come south.

By December of 2005, though I was junior at work, I was also learning pretty quickly on the job. Because we were an NBC affiliate, if something big happened in our little market—Yuma was home to about eighty-five thousand people at the time—

they'd dial us in. It meant other stations were sometimes talking to Alexis and me about what had happened, and we were appearing on top ten networks to talk about Yuma's big news. A couple months after the jet crashed into those backyards, President George W. Bush came to Yuma to address the illegal immigration issues there. I hadn't realized until then how much of an issue the US-Mexico border was. My experience with a border was crossing over the Canada-US border with clothes we'd bought at the Gap. This was a whole new border issue in Yuma. It was literally life-or-death.

Every morning it was a new story. About people dying trying to cross the desert. People getting caught smuggling illegal immigrants across the border. About the Minutemen, who were citizens that took matters into their own hands and patrolled the border themselves, with rifles. If you drove to Phoenix or San Diego, there was a checkpoint by border patrol, and they'd search your car. I had colleagues and friends who'd routinely get stopped in their own country by border patrol, and that was so foreign to me. I don't mean to sound ignorant, but I hadn't realized the extent of these border and immigration issues.

People would try to illegally sneak their way into Yuma every day, contending with the desert and the hot sun. It was unbelievable. Border patrol would find people stuffed in trunks of cars. They would cram people in there. Families with young kids tried to cross over in 120-degree heat.

There were countless drop houses—places illegal immigrants would stay after they'd been smuggled across. People would move between different drop-house locations until they made it to their destination. Border patrol would find a drop house, and unless it was a significant bust of, say, ten or more people plus the smugglers they were paying to sneak them across, it often wouldn't even make the news. If there were just two people, we probably wouldn't report on that, depending on the news day, particularly if there was a lot going on. And there was almost always a lot going on in Yuma.

This was all eye-opening to me, being in an environment with daily news that was important. I'd worked at a radio station, but everything there was pretty static. There wasn't breaking news, reasons to really be on your toes like in Yuma. The chatter there was constant. The police radio was going at all hours. I'd get there at two thirty a.m. and there'd be an accident announced three minutes later on the scanner we had in the newsroom that we'd have to cover. And because it was such a small operation, and so short-staffed, we had to do everything. We were oftentimes filling multiple roles.

Though so much of what we covered was important, it honestly felt like kids were running the station. The control room would usually consist of a director, TV operator, audio operator, teleprompter operator, and you'd hope for two camerapeople. At least twice a week, two people in the control room just wouldn't show up. Sometimes the camera operator wasn't there, for unknown reasons. They were probably getting paid less than I was. "I slept in" was probably (definitely) the reason they were missing.

Some days, Alexis and I would do the entire hour-and-a-half show ourselves. We would edit it together, usually using clips from the evening show the night before. Alexis reported the weather every twenty minutes or so. If the teleprompter operator didn't show up, then we'd have to roll our own teleprompter, using a foot pedal to control the words we'd see on the screen in front of us, so we could keep our arms free to gesture. If Alexis was holding the foot pedal, I would slide my foot over hers when she got up to report the weather. Seriously! It was pretty hilarious, and hard to remain professional.

If one of us accidentally took our foot off the pedal, the teleprompter would run all the way back up the top of the script and we'd have to ad-lib while we found the right spot in our script. *Yikes.* That happened a couple of times. "We're working on a traffic update," I'd say as we scrambled to get the teleprompter back to its rightful place.

Because of the absences, and because of our minuscule staff, I learned a lot, and quickly. And the best part is that I got opportunities to work in sports, too. KYMA had this *Friday Night Football Show*, and it always needed extra bodies to gather footage. My hand was always up to help out. *Friday Night Football* became my beat. Not only did I want to work in sports, but I remembered what I'd been told by my friend Jared, who worked at the Score in Toronto, to only take jobs in sports. This was my way to make sure I kept that door open.

I'd go out with a camera as far away as El Centro, California, about an hour-and-a-half drive. I'd get any footage I could from the game—big touchdowns, huge celebrations—then hurry back to the KYMA station to edit the clips and run them on air. I felt a rush being near the action on field, catching the big plays on camera, then hustling back to make sure people got the news about their favourite local high school football team.

I rarely caught the end of the game, because the show was at ten p.m. and I had to get back to the studio and edit and prepare the clips. Then I'd call in and get the score so we could include that in the show. Americans take their football seriously, and we all took our jobs seriously to get them what they needed. I was far more comfortable working in football than I was on immigration issues, too.

I was learning everything on the fly. But never once did I question that this is what I wanted to do with my life. At every turn I thought: *This is awesome, look how much I'm learning.* And at times, I felt like this was the big time. For instance, I'd throw to a national news reporter and get her update on Hurricane Katrina. It was important work.

I also enjoyed starting over on my own. No one in Yuma or the desert knew what my past life was like. No one was confused by my career change because they didn't know me as an engineer. I felt like the pressure had been relieved. I often thought about what Paul had asked me before I got into broadcasting: "If you lived somewhere else, what would you want to do?" And this right here, this was it. I was doing what I wanted to do, away from home.

The Golden Baseball League (GBL) season had started and the Yuma Scorpions were playing out of Desert Sun Stadium, where the San Diego Padres used to host spring training. The GBL was an independent league with teams based in the western parts of Canada and the US, as well as northwest Mexico, and while the GBL wasn't affiliated with Major League Baseball, some big names played in the league over the years. Rickey Henderson even came to town in 2005 with the San Diego Surf Dawgs and I got to watch him! The crowd to see him was enormous, and Rickey played it right up. He was forty-six years old. The man had once called himself "the greatest of all time," and he had the attitude to back it up. The big gold chains. The swagger. The powerful hits. He was still so fast, too. Rickey was known for not only being the best leadoff hitter in MLB history but for stealing bases better than anybody in the game.

The next season, Jose Canseco played in the league with the Chico Outlaws, and the crowds absolutely exploded when his team played the Scorpions. Speaking of the Scorpions, I dated a member of the team, Will, a lefty pitcher, for a couple months. He was a tall guy from Florida. Yuma was the best baseball he'd ever play. We were never serious, but it was fun. Meanwhile, Alexis was dating a pitcher with the Chicago Cubs. They got engaged, and later married. I felt like Alexis lite, dating this guy on the Scorpions.

Alexis and I had fun away from work, but we also had a lot of laughs at the office. And it wasn't always serious news we were covering. We'd get emails about opportunities to talk to celebrities about a new product, or a book, and we'd do those interviews on air. Colin Cowie was doing a press tour for his book *Colin Cowie's Extraordinary Weddings: From a Glimmer of an Idea to a Legendary Event*. He'd appear on the TV behind us, and we'd dial in and interview him. "Tell us about the most exotic, over-the-top party you've planned," I'd say. He told us about how he wanted to enable people to plan weddings, and how his book was a go-to guide. This was a big show for us. A way to be big-time. Colin Cowie was a big name.

But the coolest author we ever talked to was . . . Fabio! Seriously. Remember him? I got the email that he was doing a press tour for his book and I ran straight to Alexis: "Oh my gosh: We could interview Fabio!" I told her. We jumped up and down and high-fived. *The* Fabio. Model. Actor—he'd been in that movie, *Dude, Where's My Car?*—and now, an author! Getting to speak to him was awesome. "Fabio—how are you?" That was legitimately my first question to him. "Ladies, wonderful to join you this morning!" he said, charming as ever, even though he'd probably done forty interviews before this one on the press tour. The excitement level in the lead-up to that interview, and during that interview, was through the roof. It felt so big for our small-town market.

We'd get off the air every morning at seven, and then the *Today* show would come on. Not that we ever interacted with the hosts of the *Today* show, but it came on right after ours. It made us feel like we mattered. The *Today* show's hosts in 2006 were Matt Lauer and Katie Couric, and when Katie left and Meredith Vieira stepped in, she immediately did an amazing job. She was so much fun. Everyone was worried about who'd fill Katie's shoes, and Meredith made any worry vanish instantly.

And for me, because I was watching these hosts every morning, it was my first realization that when you invited TV hosts and broadcasters into your home, it actually felt like they were your friends. That was the first time in my life that I thought about it and it hit me: I felt like I had a connection with these people. I liked their banter. I kind of knew them. I finally understood why people at home get so passionate about certain stations or personalities, because it feels like you know the people on camera. And I wanted to be one of those people. Someone viewers felt they knew and could trust. Someone viewers cared about.

Al Roker was definitely one of those broadcasters. From seven to nine a.m., he would check in with weather updates every half hour. He threw to every NBC affiliate in the US, and he would do the weather across the country, and then he'd get specific and cut to every little studio. He'd cut to KYMA in Yuma, to one of us on a green screen, and we'd announce either the five-day forecast or the twenty-four-hour forecast. We never got to interact with Al, and he couldn't see us and didn't know who we were, but we were basically talking to him, if you ask me.

"Here's what's happening in your neck of the woods," Al would say, and either Alexis or I would fill him in on Yuma. "It's nice and sunny here, Al," I'd say on a sweltering 109-degree day. "It's warm." I was really getting the hang of it.

I may not have actually known Al or Meredith, but I did have actual friends, I swear. In very little time, I got tight with the other reporters at KYMA because we were together so often, hustling and always so busy at work. We had to be close to work together that often on constant deadlines.

The morning-show crew and evening news gang didn't see much of each other during the week because of our schedules—I was going to bed when they were getting ready for their six p.m. show. But the morning staff even hung out on our off days. A few of the other girls and I would take road trips to San Diego or Phoenix. We even made it to Vegas once and danced for hours. I gambled for the first time and won five bucks (USD!) on the slots. I cashed in and that was that, and we hustled back in time to go to bed early on Sunday so we'd could get to the station at two thirty on Monday morning.

There wasn't a lot of extra spending money for us in those days, so we would try to stay with friends of Alexis's—she had buddies scattered around the country. And we definitely weren't flying, any-way. It was all about road trips and how far we could go by car in a short amount of time. I bonded most with the other women at the station because we had so much to talk about, so much shared experience, and it helped to know that we were all going through the same thing: trying to break into this industry together. KYMA had some powerful women on staff, including Alexis. You knew that woman was driven, that she'd be going places. It was motivating to know I had colleagues like her.

And in time, back at home in Yuma, Alexis and I became—well, not famous like Edgar—but recognizable. Walking around town, people started to recognize us. It helped that there were so many parades in Yuma and in nearby El Centro, where KYMA also had a bureau. We were always in parades and festivals in both cities.

I think Yuma has to be the parade and festival capital of America. Just trust me on that. We had a parade for lettuce, of course. Hundreds of people marched along, dressed like lettuce. Americans, I learned, love their holidays, and they celebrate them all. In Yuma they not only did the classics like Thanksgiving, Christmas, and Memorial Day, but they also had a parade of lights in late December, which was really cool—they'd light up the desert sky. That was one of my favourites. There was also the Medjool Date Festival—those dates were grown in the Southwest, so they were a big deal. Obviously they needed a date festival, right?

We anchors and reporters would be on KYMA floats for every single parade. I remember thinking it was a joke the first time they told me that was part of the job. "Really? We're *in* the parade?" Yep. Because we were part of the community, which was really cool. So we'd ride around in a big white cube van. We'd sit on top, or walk alongside it, and wave and smile. It was hilarious. Ridiculous. We'd be with the van while people dressed up as lettuce for the lettuce parade or turkeys for the Thanksgiving parade or elves for the Christmas parade or dates for the Medjool Date Festival walked along with us.

I loved the recognition. I loved that people knew who I was. I found the attention awesome, and it was never bad. This was before the days of social media, when people tell you whatever they want whenever they want because they can hide behind a screen. Back then, I'd be recognized around town by people who would say things like: "Hi, Evanka, I love your show!" I really enjoy talking to and meeting new people, and it made me feel like I was famous. Like a celebrity, even though I'd never reach Edgar's level. It's a really cool feeling, and I'd be lying if I said it didn't make my head grow a little bit bigger to be recognized like that. A local would see me eating breakfast and come up and say: "I loved that segment on Fabio's book!" I thought it was so much fun to be recognized for my work.

I even started to get some fan mail at the station. People would write me a card and say things like: "Evanka, you bring such great energy to the broadcast. I'd love to meet you one day." It was amazing. My fan mail was pretty sparse compared to Edgar's and Alexis's—Alexis even got some mail from the local jail, and it was pretty creepy when it came to guys in there who had comments about her looks. I never got jail mail myself, and I was more than okay with that.

"Evanka, be careful!" Mum told me time and time again. "I am being careful, I swear!" I'd tell her over and over.

All the recognition from viewers helped me feel more confident as an anchor. But the biggest factor in getting me to a confident and comfortable place on the air was definitely Alexis. She was quick and witty and always had a great response to everything when we were live. "It's warm today," I'd say, and Alexis would fire back with "But you know who's hot? Fabio! And we'll be talking to one of the most famous models in the world next about his new project! You don't want to miss this." She was just so quick.

Being paired with Alexis helped me learn to respond and keep the show fun and engaging and informative. I felt like I was start-ing to get it. "That's the date set for an upcoming trial," Alexis would say. "And speaking of dates, that big date festival is coming up tomorrow," I'd say, transitioning to our next topic, cool as a cucumber.

About a year into my contract, in 2006, I learned another thing about journalism: It can be competitive as anything. Some of my colleagues had agents, and as their contracts were expiring in Yuma, they were all applying for jobs in various markets. Everybody wanted good stuff for their résumé tape, and if anyone was approaching the end of their two-year contract, I started to see they were really in it for themselves.

Yuma was the first time I saw things get catty among reporters and anchors. They'd get territorial about what they'd be covering, fighting for the big stories before they moved on to their next job.

Luckily, I had started a good six months after anyone else, so I was watching everyone else fight over stories. Two of the anchors warred over a big immigration story and who would report on it. There was also a bit of a rift between the morning and night show. We didn't feel supported in the morning, since we were leanly staffed and had a longer show, but the night show definitely got more eye-balls. That contributed to the dynamic at work, too.

Landing a job at a network ranked ninety-eighth was an accom-plishment. But you wanted a top twenty network. We all aspired to be like this former KYMA anchor named Veronica de la Cruz, who was on CNN in Las Vegas. Everyone talked about her, and we knew about Veronica because the news directors who had been there the longest told us all about her career. "Oh my gosh, she used to work in Yuma," we'd say. We put Veronica on a pedestal even though no one there actually knew her. Veronica was the stuff of lore. The minor leaguer that had made it to the Bigs.

The hustling helped, for sure. Just under two years into her time in Yuma, Alexis left for a job in Phoenix. That was a huge deal, since Phoenix ranked in the top fifteen in the country. And it was no surprise to me or anybody else at KYMA. We knew Alexis would move up quickly and be a star. She was an absolute natural. She had something special.

Me? I felt like I had to work toward moving up in the broadcasting world. And I didn't mind that whatsoever. If I thought about how long I'd actually been in journalism, it was less than a couple of years, and I'd already learned so much. I could literally run a morning show by myself. I also had my well-established routine by then: get to the station at two thirty a.m., do the noon show, take a nap, work out, then go to bed at six thirty p.m. so I could be up and at 'em at two a.m. again. Party on the weekends with my colleagues. Rinse. Repeat. I loved my life. And the most pleasant surprise was that I hadn't seen a snake yet, even a year into my stay. I was successfully avoiding that nightmare.

In April of 2006, the network was doing what it calls "sweeps." Sweeps happen twice a year with US networks, and it's a monthlong period where stations spend a lot of money because ratings are about to come out and they want to boost the station's standing. Reporters are all encouraged to pitch big features, and I had one in mind.

My colleague and friend Jeane was dating a guy named Michael Johnson, and he worked as a trainer for pro athletes. I'd gotten to know Michael well, since I spent lots of time with Jeane, who worked at the station as a sports reporter. Michael knew I was from Toronto, and he mentioned he'd been working with Blue Jays catcher Bengie Molina. "I actually train Bengie in the off-season—he stays in Yuma, because his wife and kids still live here," Michael told me. That immediately set off alarms in my head: *I should pursue a story on Bengie!* The timing was perfect, too: I was heading home in April for a friend's wedding in Toronto and I could interview him there about his hometown of Yuma.

The next day, I pitched the story to my news director, Robert. "It'll be great—I'll head to my hometown to talk to Bengie about his hometown," I said. "Great," Robert replied. "Go for it."

Little did I know, this interview would be the most important moment of my career. It would change my life forever.

Hitting My Stride

"How was hockey?" That's my new favourite question to be asked. It's what Adam asks me at the end of his workday on Tuesday, because that's the day I have my skills skate. It's the first thing Ken asks me as I walk into the studio on Tuesday nights, because he knows I was plugging away on the ice earlier that day.

Ken's next question is always: "Did you get pucks in deep?" Nobody—I mean *nobody*—likes talking about pucks in deep more than Ken Reid. And honestly, I usually do get a puck or two in deep, because at this point in the short scrimmages we sometimes have at the end of skills sessions, I'm often dumping the puck in, just firing it down the ice. That's because I get scared once it touches my stick and I basically give it away. Yes, my game is a work in progress, but I have to say, discussing that progress is so much fun. I've been talking about hockey at Sportsnet for more than fifteen years now, and not a day goes by when the game doesn't come up at least once. But talking about my own hockey career? That's new, and I love it. I love the idea that I'm working on a skill for myself.

Adam's most frequent question a couple of months into my hockey skills skates is: "Did you raise the puck today?" Not quite, but I'm so close, and I've been working on my wrist shot with Coach Ethan. I'll let Adam know as soon as that wrister is flying. I'm working on my crossovers, too, and right over left is coming along. The other way needs major work. But let's remember I just started playing this game, and I'm only three months into my skills sessions. There's so much to learn.

If I compare myself to Adam, he's been playing since he was five years old, and has been in a weekly beer-league skate his whole adult life. It's nice to have a common interest, even though we don't play on the same ice. George always asks his dad about his hockey games, and he's started asking me about my skates, too.

"Are you fast, Mom?"

"Uhh . . . I'm getting there, Georgie!" I tell him.

"Want to race me?" he asks.

"Who do you think would win, George?"

"Me!" he says, jumping up and down.

Yeah, he's probably right. George is only five, but let's face it, he's been playing months longer than I have.

It's so fun for our family to have hockey to talk about. It's just really nice for Adam and me to have a new shared interest to discuss. Besides kids. Besides work.

I'm also telling Adam a bit about the women I'm meeting on the ice and becoming friends with. MJ and I often sit beside each other in the dressing room, and we talk about anything and everything. How our games are progressing, about her daughter, her grandkids, George and Blake, what we're up to vacation-wise, what we're eating. You name it, we talk about it.

And this week, MJ surprised me in the best way when she told me about her latest flame. It's a man she met decades ago, who'd moved away, but had recently returned home. They'd run into each other at the grocery store, and maybe there was a chance to reignite. "MJ!" I said, pressing her for details. "When's your first date?"

"We're going to have coffee next week," she told me.

My first question at our skate next week will obviously be: "How was the date?" And my follow-up: "Will there be a second date?"

Another friend at hockey is Robyn, who knows my sister, Kay. We've been chatting about books we're reading, and recently she recommended *The Midnight Library* by Matt Haig, which I just finished reading. "Robyn, I *loved it*," I tell her. "I can't wait for your next recommendation." I'm also learning what to do—and not do—when it comes to maintaining your equipment. Last week I was tying up my skates and one of the women was talking about how she needed her skates sharpened. My ears perked up. "How do you know when it's time?" I sheepishly asked.

Three ladies immediately gave me their thoughts, and a woman named Jane even rushed over to me. "You can feel your blades. If you run your nail along the side, you can tell," she said. "Let me feel yours." As she grabbed my blade, she ran it across her thumbnail and declared: "Yep, you're overdue."

Phew. Thank you, Jane, for coming to my rescue. Is this why I continue to fall on the ice? Is this why I can't stop or skate backward, because all this time I was skating on dull blades? No, that isn't the culprit, but it's a good lesson and a reminder I've got to keep them sharp.

One of the best parts of this experience so far is that the women who intimidated me on day one with all their experience on the ice are now helping to improve my skills. They're answering my questions, even offering up praise and advice if they think I need either.

Last week, this woman, Trudy, was so complimentary of me after our skate. "You're tough to get around," she said. "You're tall and you have a long stick, and you're using that to your advantage!"

Oh my gosh, Trudy, tell me more! I could barely speak after that. My jaw dropped. "Thank you!" I gushed. I couldn't wait to brag to Adam and Ken that I'm "tough to get around." When girlfriends ask me what's new, my latest answer will be: "My wrist shot is a work in progress, and Trudy says I'm tough to get around."

I talk hockey a lot with my girlfriends, since it's my new and exciting hobby. The other day, my friend Rachel asked if I could go for coffee on Tuesday morning. "I can't," I told her, "I have hockey."

"What?" she said with a huge smile on her face, her eyes wide as saucers. "Evanka, I used to play hockey in high school, but it's been *years* since I laced up. When do you play—I'd love to sign up. That sounds like so much fun!"

I tell Rachel all about the league, about the skills sessions, when everything runs, who she'll meet, what she'll learn. "You'll love Coach Ethan," I tell her. When I run into the league's founder, Liz O'Brien, I let her know that I've found a new recruit. I'm basically a scout now, too.

Welcome to the Big Leagues

Deep breaths, Osmak. Deep breaths.

It was August of 2006, and I was standing on the Rogers Centre turf. "I'm Evanka, from KYMA in Yuma," I told one of the Blue Jays PR staffers as I held out my hand for a shake. "I'm here to interview Bengie Molina?"

"That's right," he said with a smile. "Bengie's almost done warming up, and then I'll bring him over."

My heart was racing because it was almost showtime. My camera guy, Chris, and I were ready to go, set up along the third baseline. But there's something about pitching a big feature that involves travel, and feeling pressure for it to go well. That's what made the lead-up to this interview scary. And this was my first big one! I kept reminding myself to take deep breaths. In and out. In and out.

It didn't help much. I tried hard not shake, but that didn't work, either. I had just walked through the dugout for the first time. I'd been in this ballpark dozens of times for games as a fan, watching baseball and basketball. But this was different. I dressed as sharply as possible, in a navy-blue blazer with some off-white pants. I tried to act like I'd been here before. Confidence is a magic trick, right?

What really stood out to me is the fact that as I looked around, I knew: This is where I wanted to be. Where I should be. The big time! My eyes were wide-open. It brought me back to all the amazing experiences I'd had in the Rogers Centre as a kid. Just imagine coming to the ballpark every day for your job. Imagine being even closer to that atmosphere and being paid for it. And as I was thinking all this, working myself through deep breaths, Bengie walked over, smiling.

He greeted me and mentioned Yuma, and just like that, the weight lifted off my shoulders. Bengie couldn't have been more accommodating and he worked with my questions, giving nice, detailed answers. He told me he loved living in the desert. We talked about his favourite spots to go to in Yuma, and his family. Bengie's younger brothers, José and Yadier, were also MLB catchers, so we talked about their family and how they got into baseball and all ended up playing the same position. Then we got into his time in Toronto with the Blue Jays.

Once the camera turned off, Bengie and I talked some more about our favourite Yuma spots. He told me I had to try El Charro Cafe. I promised I would when I got back.

To say I was flying high after that interview is an understatement. I was on top of the world, honestly. My first big feature was a success! And that's probably why I felt like I had the confidence to do what came next.

A group of reporters was standing near the dugout watching batting practice, all chatting together. Jerry Howarth was there, and I recognized him from watching and listening to Blue Jays games over the years. I also recognized Jamie Campbell, who did play-by-play for Sportsnet's Blue Jays broadcasts.

"I should introduce myself to someone over there," I told Chris. We were huddled over by the third baseline, feeling shy. "I mean, this is where I want to be, in sports," I said. "This is so cool."

"I don't know," Chris replied. "I probably wouldn't bother. They're all busy preparing for the game."

I looked at the reporters and they were all laughing as they stood around on the field. They didn't seem all that busy to me. So I decided to go for it. It's not that I'm shy, but it's intimidating approaching a group of men in a position I want to be in. I needed a blast of courage to get myself to go chat up strangers. And on this day, I had it, because my interview went so well.

I walked over to Jamie Campbell, and I felt like I knew him already, because I watched Blue Jays games religiously on Sportsnet whenever I was home. I was over there before I could talk myself out of it. "Hi, Jamie, I just wanted to introduce myself. I'm Evanka Osmak," I told him. "I'm actually from around here, from Oakville. But I'm working for a network in Yuma, in Arizona." Jamie smiled and said, "Cool." I told him I was working on a feature on Bengie. "He's a great guy," Jamie said.

I told Jamie a bit about the interview, and that I'd been working mostly in news, but wanted to make the jump to sports. "This isn't for a job or anything, and I've got another year left on my contract," I said. "But do you mind if I send you my demo tape? I'd love to get any advice you might have about working in sports. That's my dream job."

Jamie was so great about it. "Absolutely," he said, and he pulled out a piece of paper and wrote not only his mailing address, but the address of his news director, Mike English, on it. "Send it to both of us, if you want," Jamie said.

"Thank you so much! I really appreciate it," I told him. "It was so nice to meet you."

When I walked back over to join Chris, I wasn't shaking anymore. I felt comfortable. And truthfully, I also felt really proud of myself. I'd gone outside my comfort zone and introduced myself, and even if it didn't lead to something great down the road, it couldn't hurt, right? I felt so thankful that journalism brought that out of me, the courage to say hi or start a conversation. It's something you often have to do during interviews on the air. You never know where conversations might lead you.

But here's the thing: Returning to Canada didn't seem like a path I wanted to explore. No, thank you. That's why I made it clear to Jamie that I wasn't looking for a job at Sportsnet, because I truly wasn't. I didn't want to come back to the harsh winters. I loved the sun in Arizona.

I headed back to Yuma a couple of days later after partying at my friend Sarah's wedding, visiting with family, and hanging out with Tato and Mum. I edited my Bengie Molina story, and I felt so proud of it. It was definitely my greatest contribution ever to KYMA. And such a unique story for our network, too.

"Evanka, you really nailed this one," my news director, Robert, told me. "Congratulations—this was a great idea."

The trip home was a success from every standpoint. And while I was glad I had met Jamie Campbell, I wasn't going to follow through on my promise to send demo tapes to him or his news director, whatever the heck his name was. I wondered what the point would be, since I was dead set on making it in the US, in some sunny state.

I only found out later that the guys I was meant to send my

demo tape to in Toronto—Jamie Campbell and his news director, Mike English—had actually been trying to track me down.

Jamie told me this story, and we laughed about it a year later, after we'd become friends. He'd been in the middle of hosting a dinner party with his family, and he got an email from Mike asking: "Do you know any women who are looking for a job on air?" Jamie remembered me because we'd met just a few days earlier. I wonder if my awkwardness made it even more memorable. Hey, sometimes awkwardness comes in handy!

"A woman came up to me during a game earlier this week," Jamie wrote back. But he couldn't for the life of him remember my name or what network I was with. He did recall I was from Oakville, and working somewhere in Arizona. Jamie googled a few keywords like "anchor," "Oakville," and "Arizona" and scrolled through the photos that turned up. "Luckily, yours was right there on the first page and I recognized you," Jamie told me. "If you were on the second page, I wouldn't have pressed 'next.' We never would've found you."

You can't blame Jamie—he wanted to get back to his dinner party. Thank goodness I made page one. Jamie fired back an email to Mike and said: "There's your girl. Find her or not, I'm going back to my party."

After that, the good people at Sportsnet were able to track down my KYMA email address. In July of 2006, I got an email from a guy named Mike English from a Sportsnet account. "Hello, Evanka," he wrote. "I heard you were looking for a job in Toronto. If you are, get back to me."

But here's the thing: It had been four months since I introduced myself to Jamie Campbell. Four months since I misplaced that piece of paper with their addresses on it. I didn't remember Mike's name. I was pretty sure this email was a hoax.

I decided to check to make sure this was all a joke, and if it wasn't, I figured going through an interview process for a job I didn't want would be a valuable experience once I landed an interview for a job I did want. Following up on this Sportsnet email, if it wasn't from a robot, seemed like a good idea. I wrote to my old friend from high school, Jared, who worked at the Score. I asked him if Mike English was legitimate, and Jared confirmed that he was.

So I wrote back to Mike and told him I was interested. I sent along my demo tape, which definitely included my crown jewel of an interview with Bengie Molina. A lot of time passed after my initial email exchange with Mike, but eventually Sportsnet flew me to Toronto for an interview in January of 2007.

If I had known what this job was going to turn into, I would have been *so* nervous to do that interview. I would have known that it was my absolute dream job. The kind of job I'd been working toward, the kind of job I didn't expect I'd get until much later in my career. A sports anchor for a major network. Wow. But because it was in Toronto, and Toronto is home to winters and snow, I figured this wasn't for me. Honestly, that's what I was thinking. I know, I know: *Osmak, give your head a shake!* But because I didn't want the job, I was calm and cool for the interview. I didn't feel pressure. And luckily, it worked in my favour.

First, I did a screen test. I sat behind a desk and read a script on the main stage—a huge stage surrounded with lights and cameras, all of them focused on me. I went through highlights, which was a piece of cake. Golf and hockey were in the highlight package, two of my favourite sports. I talked about eagles and hat tricks, and it felt so comfortable and fun. I think I came off like I knew my stuff. I found out later from a few of the camera guys working that day that Sportsnet interviewed lots of women with broadcast experience, but not many who followed sports. They were comfortable speaking into cameras, but not necessarily discussing Tiger Woods saving par on a thirty-five-foot putt to stay in contention at the PGA Championship, which he'd eventually win.

After the screen test was an interview with Sportsnet's senior director of television, Julie Borthwick. The first thing she said when I sat down was: "I went to St. Mildred's, too!" We immediately hit it off and traded school stories. She was a year younger than my sister, Kay. I felt instantly at ease around Julie. Part of it was because, honestly, I didn't expect the director of television in sports to be a woman, and maybe it was this feeling I shared with Julie that we had this common interest, in addition to the fact we'd gone to the same school. It was an immediate bond. When the interview finished, Julie invited me to lunch. It got me thinking: *Maybe I'm getting this job.* But I still didn't think I wanted it.

Being home during the interview process was a blast. I surprised my girlfriend Betsy for her twenty-eighth birthday. I stayed with Mum and Tato, in my old bed, in their newly built home. Jeannie made my favourite breakfast. It was so comfortable and so nice to be around friends and family who'd known me basically my whole life.

I flew to Yuma late Sunday night and the email job offer came through from Mike English a few days later. "Thank you so much!" I replied "I'm going to take a few days to think about it, and I'll get back to you soon." I immediately picked up the phone and called my parents to tell them I had a job as an anchor at Sportsnet—if I wanted it.

"Mum and Tato, I don't know, I'm pretty set on staying in Arizona, or around here," I said. "I really love the warm weather."

"Evanka, don't be silly!" Jeannie said. "This is a fantastic opportunity."

"And it's sports, what you always wanted," Tato added.

Well, my parents did have a point.

I just had to figure it out on my own. And when I stopped and realized what I was being offered at Sportsnet—that national attention, covering the biggest sports in the world—it was an absolute no-brainer. Money was a factor, too, because I'd be making more than I was in Yuma. I'd be on probation for three months until I was officially an employee, but still, I could actually go out for dinner. Buy coffee from Starbucks without thinking about how much money I'd have left over for lunch. It was a huge leap. And I'd get a wardrobe allowance on top of that. A clothing consultant. I'd have my hair and makeup taken care of by someone else. Even better than the money was the exposure and the idea of returning home to be with family and friends.

Four days after I got the offer, I wrote Mike, accepting the job, and I told him how excited I was to start at Sportsnet.

I signed the contract, and Mike said he hoped I could start a couple of weeks later. I figured I'd be able to, but once I talked it over with Robert, my news director at KYMA, I realized that wasn't possible, because I was bound to my contract and I had to work until the end of it. KYMA only let us out of contracts if we moved to a bigger network in the US, and because I was leaving to work in Canada, Robert decided to be a stickler—it came across as a power-trip move, honestly—and make me work the remaining six weeks of my contract. Luckily, Sportsnet agreed to wait.

Those six weeks took forever. It didn't help that my whole original Yuma crew had moved on to other opportunities already. I had to wait until the end of March to officially leave Yuma behind. It's that feeling in school when grades have already been calculated, but you still have an assignment to hand in, so you don't put in much effort; you just plod toward the finish line. And at KYMA, I started to see the cracks even more. Two people didn't show up to work one morning. I didn't really need to hustle during my last weeks because I already had a job secured, but at least I showed up. Once I realized what was waiting for me back home, I wanted to peace out of Yuma.

What occurred to me, too, is how much I'd missed out on since I'd been away from home. Listen, I wouldn't change my experience in Yuma for anything. I learned so much there and I felt happy with my career. But I'd be lying if I didn't admit that I felt way behind in my personal life.

I was twenty-six, and four of my friends were already engaged. So was my sister, Kay, to this gem of a guy named Chris. I was going to be a bridesmaid three times in the summer of 2007, including for my sister. All my friends had significant others. They were even talking about having kids. I knew I didn't want kids, that they wouldn't fit my lifestyle. But I did really want to get married. I'm the romantic type: Big party. White dress. Speeches. Dancing. Pictures to remember those moments forever. I'll admit, I wanted all that with the man of my dreams. But I hadn't met him yet. And wasn't I getting a little old, at twenty-six? Had I missed my window?

"Lara, dating sucks. Where do I even meet someone these days?" I asked my friend, and not for the first time. Lara always reassured me: "Oh, it'll come." *Yeah, easy enough for you to say, you're already engaged.* And that's what everyone told me, that I'd find a great guy soon. But would I? My fingers were crossed.

Truthfully, a lot was up in the air for me, even though I was moving home, and I'd be surrounded by family and a lot of my best friends. I still didn't know what the next phase would look like, but I had high hopes for my career and for my personal life.

Team Player

It strikes me every time I walk into North Toronto Memorial Arena: This place *feels* like hockey. It's a character-filled old rink, nearly sixty years old. The logo at centre ice includes the rink's birth year, 1965. Most of the inside of the arena is painted green, including the wooden benches that make up the stands. There are banners on the walls for NHL stars like Eric Lindros and Tom Wilson, who grew up playing here.

It's pretty inspirational. On the broadcast the other night we were talking about Wilson, who plays for the Capitals, and of course I pointed out, "We both got our start at North Toronto Memorial, Ken." I mean, we have so many similarities when it comes to our hockey careers, Tom Wilson and me.

We both play for big trophies, for one. In the lobby of the arena you'll find the Sister Sports grand prize, the Skate Sister Cup. The winners of the Wednesday league get their names engraved on it, just like the Stanley Cup. Tom Wilson won the Stanley Cup in 2018. Maybe 2026 is my year for the Skate Sister Cup.

I'm about to find out more about it. I just got off the ice, with plans to sit down for coffee with Liz O'Brien afterward. She's the founder of Sister Sports—the organization that offers not just hockey, but also volleyball and pickleball to women over the age of thirty-five or so. I'd talked to Liz a few times since I signed up, but I wanted to learn more about her, and how she started Sister Sports.

As soon as we sit down, it's clear: Liz is awesome. She grew up in Vancouver playing tons of sports, including field hockey, but never hockey on ice. She picked it up when she was thirty-nine (so young, compared to forty-one) and immediately fell in love with it, exactly the way I did. By then she had four kids who were school-age, and had left her very busy job as an investment banker. A friend of hers had signed up for a learn-to-play-hockey class, and convinced Liz to join.

"For me, it was like that reawakening," Liz says. "Being on a team, being competitive—it had been so long since I'd been on a team. The last time was when I was an undergrad in university, play-ing field hockey."

"It was even longer for me!" I tell her. "High school field hockey!"

Liz and I hit it off immediately. And like me, she loved her in-troduction to hockey, but wanted something closer to home. That's why she started Skate Sister when she was forty. Liz had a back-ground in the sport because she'd managed one of her kids' hockey teams, and knew that ice time in Toronto was both expensive and in demand. She also knew mid-morning ice wasn't as in demand, and that women with young kids and flexible jobs might be able to make it work. Liz started at first recruiting friends and neighbours, and the league began with hour-long Friday-morning scrimmages. She reached out to the day care at the local community centre, and timed the ice so that parents could drop their kids off and come play afterward. Nearly everyone was an absolute beginner, though most had experience playing some kind of sport. Lots of hockey moms wanted to give it a try, too.

"There's a lot of women who either were home raising kids and had a little window of time to exercise, or women who had part-time jobs or worked for themselves and could fit it in, so it just kind of worked," she said. "We grabbed that time and people came out of the woodwork. There were more women who could make that work than we thought. And now we've got this whole daytime program going."

She started with about thirty women who'd scrimmage on Friday mornings at North Toronto Memorial. Soon after, Liz found other groups across Toronto playing in different rinks, discovering that women across the city over thirty had been finding hockey and falling in love with it. She wanted to cultivate more of that because she'd felt such a surge of energy being around like-minded women, finding this new, fun, fast, and exciting hobby. She wanted to provide opportunities for more women to join the fun.

"It occurred to me: There's enough women doing this informally. If we created a league for this, I bet people would join," she says. "I had a lot of pent-up desire to do something other than being a mom, and it occurred to me everything I was doing just informally actually was a small business waiting to happen."

It was back in 2016 that Liz founded Skate Sister, so it's coming up on a decade. The program has grown to include skills sessions and A, AA, and AAA scrimmages, to draw in not just beginners, but players with more experience. There's now a four-on-four league on Fridays with eight teams, largely for beginners. There are skills classes on Tuesdays that I attend, and the Wednesday program for

A, AA, and AAA players, which I'm thinking of signing up for next (for a chance to win that Skate Sister Cup!). The goalies switch halfway through the game, so you can never pin wins or losses on them. The age ranges from about thirty to seventy-five or so. There are a handful of grandmothers in the league.

"It's a women's community," Liz says. "The stuff you hear in the locker room—everyone's going through life stuff, right? Kids and aging parents. Someone has a kid who's going through something? They find someone in the locker room who can help or knows someone who can help."

The rink is a ten-minute drive from my house, but Liz tells me some of the players drive upward of an hour to get here to play. And I get it, because it's fun and important to everyone. "The demand is there," she says, which is why the business has grown to include volleyball and, more recently, pickleball.

"Thank you, Liz," I tell her just before we say goodbye. "I think I speak for a lot of us when I say I'm so grateful that you've created this community."

As I walk out to my car, I can't help but think about my mum. I want to call her up right now and tell her about Liz and this business, because I know she'd love to hear all about it. But my mum doesn't pick up the phone anymore when I call. Speaking has become really difficult. I just wish I could hear what she had to say about the league, and about my newfound passion. I know she'd be proud that I was going all-in on an activity for myself, and not just signing George and Blake up for new experiences.

I decided to have kids later in life than many of my friends—I was thirty-six when I had George, which is not exactly what I'd call old, but society labels you a "geriatric pregnancy." I remember hearing those words used to describe me for the first time at the fertility clinic and thinking: "Oh *hell no*. It's not like I'm seventy-eight!"

My friends from high school and university had started having kids in their late twenties and early thirties. I never felt pressured to join them, mostly because I didn't think I wanted children of my own. I had two nieces and a nephew and that was plenty of children in my life, thank you very much.

It meant that for most of my adult life, I could do whatever I wanted. Friends had to worry about getting babysitters so we could have dinner, or they couldn't go on trips because of their kids. Meanwhile Adam and I were living out our best DINK—dual income, no kids—lives. If I wanted to do a nine a.m. workout class, no problem. If on Saturday night I wanted to go out for a last-minute dinner, piece of cake. All my expenses were for me. I was a responsible adult, but I didn't have to be responsible for anyone. I didn't even have a pet.

But then Adam and I decided we did want kids (I'm pretty confident he always had, but he wasn't going to let it be a deal-breaker). I came around after spending lots of time with Kay and her family, after enough Sunday family dinners with a bunch of kids running around, while I was Aunt Evanka and he was Uncle Adam. Often, we'd be at the cottage with Adam's family on a Sunday night, or with my family, and there'd be so much action with all the kids. It hit me on one of the drives back home that it was time for Adam and me to have a unit of our own. It just felt right.

But it can be easy to lose yourself in everything that having young kids entails, on top of trying to work and make a living. It can be easy to tell yourself that you don't have time, to have your mind consumed by your kids' wants and needs, and household chores and work. Adult stuff. For me, hockey is one of the disruptions to all that adult stuff.

As I've mentioned, one of my mum's passions when we were kids was designing and being creative. When my parents decided to build their dream house in 2003 on an empty lot in Oakville, it was Jeannie who took the lead. She knew exactly how she wanted the backyard to look. There was a big table for family dinners, a sitting area, a grass section for the kids to play on, and it was all encircled by flowers and trees. She wanted a big island in the kitchen, too, so we could all sit around and chat while she cooked. Jeannie had plans, and a lot of them revolved around making sure we could all be together comfortably.

She worked closely with the architect on every detail, making sure it truly was her dream house. The coffered ceilings, the brick fireplace in the kitchen nook, and the sitting area in the backyard. She would drive around different cities, flip through magazines (pre-Instagram!) looking for inspiration. Everything had to be exactly what she wanted—vintage wood floors sourced from an old barn up north, working shutters, and a chandelier that took her months to track down. And you better believe that when people walked into our house for the first time, they commented on that chandelier hanging over our dining room table. It was beautiful.

Tato wasn't involved in the planning, but he was on top of the scheduling as the house came together. Both of my parents were there every day. Cleaning up after the workers went home at night. Making sure everything was going according to plan and staying on budget. By this time, Borden had retired from the bank. And while he was still consulting, he and my mum were focused on the house.

Tato sure earned his retirement, too. Work was so busy for my dad when we were kids. He was often awake and commuting to downtown Toronto before any of us had our eyes open. And he was usually home just as we were about to sit down for a dinner Jeannie had made.

For Jeannie herself, as a stay-at-home mom, making sure she had outside interests and hobbies was always top of mind. It's why she was always gardening. Walking with friends. Having movie nights. Knitting. Playing games. Keeping her mind and body active. Keeping herself happy. She said that meant she could be a better mom and partner. She felt fulfilled.

Hockey is doing that same thing for me, and I need to tell my mum about it.

After I sit down with Liz and find out about all her work with Skate Sister, I decide to drive to Oakville to see my parents. Even if my mum can't say much, I want to tell her about Liz, and about how I'm not losing myself. Heck, I'm finding myself out on the ice.

When I arrive, I open the front door and Jeannie is sitting on the light green couch. There's a mask over her face, attached to a tube, hooked up to a machine. That machine is helping my mum breathe. It's her new accessory. I hear her cough up mucus as she takes a deep breath when she sees me come in the door.

I'm so excited to talk to my mum, to tell her about the kids, to tell her about my hockey league and all my progress on the ice. I want to let her know I'm going to switch from Tuesday skills to the Wednesday scrimmages. Yes, I'm ready for games! I decided that officially after my chat with Liz. I know she'd be proud that I'm taking her advice to heart, still pursuing something for myself.

"Mum, I'm going to start scrimmages next week—I'm signing up for the A league," I tell her. She smiles. She pulls out her pad of paper and pen and writes what I can barely read, but it looks like "Good for you!" She started writing us notes recently, at the start of December, when talking became too hard. Already her writing is becoming almost illegible; it's even loopier than it was the last time I was here. She's losing the strength required to move her hand.

The decline has been so rapid that I fear that, soon, my mum won't be able to write. Or text. Soon, she won't be able to communicate.

"Coach Ethan says my shot is really improving," I tell her as I take a seat on the couch beside her. Then I talk about my friend MJ, about George's passion for Connor McDavid, and about how Blake loves wrestling his older brother. It all makes her smile around that breathing tube hanging out of her mouth.

I'm hitting her with as much positive news as I can, but the reality is inescapable: My mum is attached to a machine, and she can't breathe on her own anymore. There's a vacancy in her eyes. She's taking in all her nutrition through a straw, since she doesn't have the power in her jaw to chew.

I excuse myself from the couch and go find Tato. He's upstairs in his room. I give him a big hug. "Want me to take Mum for a shower?" I ask. He nods and says, "Thank you, Evanks."

Kay and I have been taking our mum for showers every time we visit. It's a way we can help our dad, and it's something I know I have to do for Mum now. I go back downstairs and tell her, "It's time for a shower, Mum." I help her up from the couch and I try not to fixate on how frail she feels as I wrap my arms around her to hoist her up. I put my arm around my mum and support her as we walk slowly to the bathroom.

I remember, when my parents built this house nearly twenty

years ago, they made sure there'd be a bathroom on the main floor. "Good thing—you'll be needing that!" we kids had joked, as though they were already ninety-something and struggling on stairs. None of us thought that main-floor bathroom would be so useful quite so soon.

There's a stand-up shower in there, which is best for my mum now. Getting her in and out of a bathtub would be difficult for us both. A night earlier, I had bathed one-year-old Blake and there'd been bubbles and laughter and rubber ducks and the whole deal, and now here I was showering my mum, trying to make it seem like it's no big deal.

I'm as positive as I can be. Any sadness is put aside, and I treat giving Jeannie a shower matter-of-factly. I don't want her feeling any embarrassment whatsoever. *This is what we're doing. Let's go.*

I know she did this for me when I was a kid and now that's what I'm doing for her. I want my mum to look respectable and good, because I know that matters to her. At least I know it did once. Even if she can't recognize she's not looking her best after a couple days without a shower, I don't want her to look that way. I want her to look good.

"Here we go, Mum," I say as I remove her clothes. I can see her bones sticking out, and it's like every one of her ribs is on display. She coughs—it's hard for her to breathe without her breathing machine, which we took off for the shower. I see even more of her bones protruding as she coughs a few more times. Both of my arms are supporting her while I help her step into the shower. I have to hold my mum with at least one arm the whole time she's in there, because even though there's a little seat that we settle her into, it's still terrifying. She's so frail, and when you think about how slippery the tiles get when they're wet . . . I shudder to consider the possibilities. God forbid she slips. I've got to keep her steady. "Let's lather you up," I say, putting body wash on a loofah and lathering her up from head to toe. "Now shampoo," I say, and I work it into her dirty-blond hair before giving it a rinse. "This conditioner smells so good," I tell her as I squirt some into my hand and massage it into her hair. It's like I'm doing play-by-play for my mum's shower.

I tell her we're all done as I help her out of the shower and wrap her in a towel with a big hug. I get another towel and rub Mum's hair dry. I help her over to my parents' bed and I put her clothes on—her underwear, her socks, her sweatpants, and a matching sweatshirt. It takes at least five minutes to get all her clothes on.

"I'm going to brush your hair, Mum," I tell her. Once I'm done, I use a round brush and blow-dry it so that it's straight, and tucks under a bit at the ends. It's the way she's always worn it.

"You look great!" I say as I loop my arm around hers and help her slowly walk back to her spot on the couch. I replace the breathing machine on her face, and she clears her throat loudly, and then I watch her chest begin to rise and fall as her breathing steadies.

I tell my mum a few more stories about the kids. "George got a perfect grade on his spelling test, and Blake just started riding a balance bike. He's so fast!" Soon after, I go upstairs to say goodbye to my dad. Then I give Mum a hug and tell her goodbye. "I love you, and I'll see you soon!"

She picks up her notepad and scrawls something in big, loopy letters that are barely discernable. But I can tell what my mum is trying to say. I can see the *o* and the *v* clearly. She's written: "I love you" as best she can.

New Kid

My first day at Sportsnet was April 1, 2007—April Fools' Day. A little ominous, right?

I'd moved back in with my parents in Oakville, and I was really crushing it: twenty-six, single, living at home with Tato and Mum. Just the way I'd pictured my life. I was honestly thinking, *What the heck is my life going to look like five years from now?* It felt like a fresh start, but also like I'd taken a few steps back because I was living with my parents. But I was focused on the fresh-start part. This could be great, right?

That first day, I showered, put on minimal makeup, blow-dried my hair, and pulled on jeans, black flats, and a navy blouse. The blouse was one my mum loved. I knew to dress casually because Sportsnet as a network had recently decided to go full-time on casual Friday. It was jeans and a button-down shirt and no tie for the men, and jeans and a nice top for women. It set us apart from the competition at TSN—they wore power suits and ties. I appreciated that we at Sportsnet were taking a more casual approach to sports.

My first day was basically a meet and greet to get to know the station and see how it worked.

I drove up to the Sportsnet building in Scarborough. There it sat, right beside the TSN/CTV headquarters—the competitors. The Big Two sports networks in Canada. And I was an anchor at one of them. Wow. It hit me as I parked my car that, sure, I might be a single twenty-something who lived with her parents, but baby, when it came to my professional life, I was in the big leagues. And hopefully I was here to stay.

My new boss, Mike English, met me at reception and brought me into the studio on the main floor. I was wide-eyed, taking it all in. I saw a full crew of twenty-five people that had been there for hours, who were handling everything from sound to lighting to cameras to editing on the fly. The studio was on a giant platform that overlooked the newsroom. There were rows upon rows of young people, about 95 per cent of whom were men, waiting to cut game highlights. I saw a wall of TVs showing live programming and other screens with a static shot of the Sportsnet logo. Back then, the logo was a blue depiction of a player with a red ball, and it said "Rogers Sportsnet" underneath. Offices—like the news director's—encircled the newsroom. There were control rooms full of equipment. Soundboards. Lights. You name it. I looked around and thought: *Am I in Hollywood?*

"Evanka, this is Brad," Mike told me, snapping me out of my daze, and I shook hands with Brad Fay. He was my co-anchor. I'd done some googling and discovered he'd been working in the industry for twenty years. I'm sure he was thinking, *Great. I'm paired up with this girl who's never had a job in sports before? Or been an anchor on a national network? This should be interesting.*

I couldn't help but feel inexperienced because everything around me looked and felt so professional and polished. Then one of my on-air colleagues I'd never met before, Jason Portuondo, came over and told me I had to head over to the makeup room. "Not because you need it!" Jason said, smiling. "You're being summoned." That's where I met Corinne, the makeup artist.

"I'm so excited to meet you!" Corinne said as soon as she saw me. "I heard all about the new hire!" Corinne was in charge of all things makeup, and I'm sure she wanted to see my face to see what she was working with. As I found out later, she was so excited to get to work on another woman. Corinne was used to applying powder to the many men that worked at Sportsnet. At the time, you could count on one hand how many women were regularly on air.

Minutes later, in walked Martine Gaillard. Martine had a show coming up and she'd heard Corinne talking to me and had rushed into the makeup room to meet me. "Evanka, it's so nice to meet you!" she said, with a big smile on her face. Martine is amazing on air, with such good delivery and an incredible knowledge of sports. She's a beautiful blond anchor with phenomenal hair and a genuine smile. She's a pro, and I was looking forward to learning from her and trying to be more like her.

"We need more women in here!" she said, giving me a big hug. "You're going to love it." Corinne, Martine, and I hit it off immediately. It was clear they were both amped to have another woman in the office.

That feeling I'd had, like I didn't belong here in the big leagues? It evaporated. I loved the environment right off the bat. It was supportive, and women were supporting women.

"Let me know if you need anything at all, or if you have any questions," Martine told me. "I'm happy to help. And as you'll learn, Corinne is the best at makeup."

I couldn't wait to really get started. Not only was this a supportive environment, but it was professional on a level I'd never experienced. I spent the rest of that first day meeting everyone and getting the lay of the land, and the next day I'd be on air for the first time. My head was spinning as I drove home. Once I got there, Tato, Jeannie, and my brother, Nick, peppered me with questions. "What does the studio look like?" "Did you meet anyone famous?" "When will you be on TV?"

I had all the answers, and more. "It's huge! I met Martine Gaillard! Tomorrow!" And: "I don't have to do my own makeup! There's dozens of people working all the time. Someone is going to buy me clothes. There are people that hand you a script that someone else writes for you. There's a floor director. Someone will give me a cue when I'm on air. It's called an Interruptible Fold Back, and it's an earpiece, and that's how the control room will talk to us." That was new for me, so I'd have to get used to a producer, director, and production assistant in my ear, giving me cues, and counting down to the moment I'd be on air. "It's amazing!" I told my family. "There are so many screens. There's an assignment desk. I don't have to call a team to find out the score, or call the police to find out about the latest accident. Now it's just about sports!"

The next day was my on-air debut in the Bigs. Luckily, I wasn't thrown on the desk immediately, anchoring from day one. For the first couple of weeks, I'd be doing two-minute updates in the afternoons for Global TV, the news network Sportsnet worked with back then. I'd come in at one p.m. and that's how I'd get practice on camera.

On my first real day, I headed straight into the makeup room to see Corinne. "Have a seat," she told me, smiling, pulling out a literal suitcase of makeup. I'm not even kidding: a suitcase, and it wouldn't qualify as a carry-on. I couldn't believe how different it was already at Sportsnet. I felt like a movie star. When I did my own makeup in Yuma, I put on eye shadow, heavy eyeliner, and mascara and hoped I didn't resemble a clown. This was a whole other ball game—a luxurious, spa-like ball game. Another reminder that this was the big time. And a lesson in how much makeup you actually need for television.

Corinne started with foundation. Then some under-eye cover-up. Then white powder to set the makeup ("This is setting powder," she explained). She used *three different eye shadows.* She contoured, got it in the creases. I don't really know what she did, but she did it. Then she coloured in my eyebrows with a pencil and used a gel to set them. She contoured around my face to create angles I don't naturally have, so when the light hits, it looks like I have more prominent cheekbones than I do. Oh, the layering of makeup: It was so much! Foundations. Blushes. Setting powders. Highlighter above the cheekbones. Eyeliner on the top and bottom of the eye. Mascara. She brushed my hair and sprayed some hair spray in it so I wouldn't have fly-aways.

I sat there for forty-five minutes while Corinne worked on me. I was watching my transformation the whole time in the mirror. When she was done, I'd be lying if I didn't admit I was startled. It felt like I was wearing a lot of makeup because I was, and I looked like I was. I wasn't used to looking this done-up. But I also felt like I looked good. And ready for TV. I was definitely nervous, but since my update was less than two minutes long, I figured it would be over before I knew it.

I had memorized my script, and I could hear the producer

counting down in my ear, and then the camera light flashed on and it was showtime. I stood in front of the camera, right in our studio.

"Tonight, the Leafs take on the Senators at the Air Canada Centre, and captain Mats Sundin will look to keep his four-game point streak alive," I said, smiling at the camera. And just like that, I'd started working at Sportsnet.

Talking sports and only sports? I was loving it. And since I was doing short hits to start, getting my feet wet before the anchor shifts, I felt like it was a great introduction. I was cruising. Often in those early days I was talking about the Blue Jays, and the game coming up that night.

But then, just three days in, reality hit. Hard. Like a smack in the face. I got called into the boss's office. Mike, our news director, wanted to see me. I knew it wasn't good. It couldn't be good, because I knew I'd been screwing up. I'd been having trouble pronouncing the name of a Toronto Blue Jays pitcher. Still, it couldn't be that bad, right? I was only on the air for two minutes a day. How bad could I be?

"Evanka," Mike said, straight-faced. "You need to be better."

Gulp. I couldn't lose my dream job days after I started it. I had to be better—*had to be.*

Puck Drop

What in the heck was I thinking? I'm not ready to scrimmage. I'm not ready for a game! I've only been in skills for three months. I can't come to a full stop. How am I going to play in a game?

That's my internal monologue as I walk into the rink for my first Wednesday scrimmage session in November of 2021. The only thing that makes me feel half decent is reminding myself that my rationale is sound: I want a better workout, and I want to be part of a team. That's why I'm here, to meet and bond with other women and to be on a team and to feel tired and rewarded while I play alongside other women hoping for the same. So this is it. And I'm signed up for the A league, which is the lowest on offer by Skate Sister. Nobody plays B or C or D in this organization, just A, AA, and AAA. It's great for our confidence.

Every week we have different teams, and it's a four-on-four game, which means we get more time with the puck and more space to dangle (that's how we say stick handle). That's exciting. My expectations ahead of my first game are very, very, very low. I'm not even setting my sights on touching the puck once. My goal is much the same as it was when I got on the ice for my first skills session: Stay on my skates. Stay upright.

There are eighteen of us here this morning for the scrimmage, and Coach Ethan comes into the dressing room once we're ready to go and splits us into teams. "Osmak, you're forward," he tells me. *Phew! Defence? No thanks.* I don't need the responsibility, plus backward skating is not my strength. I can barely do that. I decide I won't start, so once the Zamboni is done and the ice is ready, I skate over to the bench.

One shift into my first-ever game, reality hits me like a ton of bricks: I'm incredibly out of shape, at least when it comes to hockey. I can ride a bike hard for an hour-long spin class, and I crush Pilates. But after skating up and down the ice a few times, I'm gasping for air. Gassed. Wiped. It's this constant back-and-forth I've never been a part of before. It's the first time I've ever really played hockey. My thighs are burning! And it's not only physically exhausting, it's mentally taxing. My mind is racing. *Where do I stand? Where do I skate? Who's getting the puck? Do I need to cover someone? Oh crap, I fell again. Okay, my teammate has the puck. Should I beeline to the net?*

And shoot: When should I go off? There's nobody monitoring my shift to make sure it isn't too long. I'm so gassed that I should go off. I stayed out for two minutes my first shift and I shave that down to one thirty for my second shift. That's as much as I can handle, especially because I'm chasing. Chasing the person with the puck. Chasing the person they pass the puck to. Chasing and never catching up.

I'm lost on the ice, too. I feel like a very old rookie who has no idea how the game of hockey is played. And honestly, this is downright shocking to me. When you watch as much hockey as I do, you think it'll just happen naturally, that you'll get out on the ice and everything will come together. I mean, I've watched Sidney Crosby and Connor McDavid enough times to know how it's done. I have been at Sportsnet for fifteen and a half years, and I watch hockey for about four hours a day. I've probably watched more than twelve thousand hours of hockey in my life. But I have no idea what to do when I'm actually on the ice.

This is a whole other game. Women are zipping by me at what seems like one hundred miles an hour. I get the puck on a broken play—the puck appears in front of me, and I skate to it. I'm skating and I nearly run into a defender on the other team because I'm not looking where I'm going, and clearly she's trying to get the puck off me, which she easily does. *Wait a minute: No one was being aggressive and digging in like that in our skills sessions!*

I skate back to the bench. It's a horrible time for a line change, because the puck is going the other way, into our defensive zone— I've seen enough bad line changes in the NHL to know better—but I'm absolutely gassed. I plunk down heavily on the bench and I check my Apple Watch. I'd set it for "hockey." I see my heart rate and calories burned and my eyes widen. In three shifts I've burned sixty calories and my heart rate is 177. My resting heart rate is typically around 55. *Holy smokes!* I'm panting. My quads are still burning. This is a workout like I've never experienced.

By the end of the game, I'm dripping with sweat. I touched the puck at least twice. I fell at least twice, too. I had no idea what I was doing out there, but I had an absolute blast. As I skate off the ice I tell myself: *I'll be even better next week.*

That's important to me, because I want that acceptance, as I assume most people do when they play a team sport. And maybe that's why I've done well playing sports in the past, because I crave that gratification. Being part of a team often gives you that feeling of being accepted. Because when you score, pass, or contribute in some way, small or large, you're part of the team. As a contributor. And these women I'm playing with are fiery and competitive and they want to play well. I feel the same way. I have a long way to go when it comes to playing well, and I tell myself I'll connect on a few passes next week. Having this first game under my belt is big. Now I (kind of) know what to expect.

Coach Ethan comes into the dressing room right after the game, while we're taking our helmets off. "Hold on to the puck, ladies! Don't be so quick to throw it away!" he reminds us. Coach is big on puck possession. "That was a great skate today—great goal, MJ!" he says, and we all cheer. MJ is beaming.

"I'm going to leave you with a quote from Aristotle," Ethan says as he's wrapping up his post-game speech. He tells us this is how he approaches both hockey and hard work more generally. Coach is big on motivational content.

"We are what we repeatedly do," Coach says. "Excellence is not an act, but a habit."

I'm smiling as I get into the car, and I immediately call Adam. "Oh my gosh, that was so much fun. Exhilarating!" I tell him. "What an amazing workout. I can't wait to talk to George and tell him that I played."

When George gets home from school I tell him I played in an actual hockey game, and I'm grinning from ear to ear. My first game.

"Did you score a goal?" he asks.

"No," I tell him.

"Oh," George says. "I scored a goal yesterday."

And he walks away.

Wow. I guess I need to score a goal to impress my five-year-old.

That night I get to the Sportsnet studio and I tell Ken all about my first game, and he's so excited for me. He also has a lot of questions. "Did you get in a fight?" No, Ken. "Did you cross-check anyone?" No, Ken. "Did you get pucks in deep?" No, Ken, but I did give it away at least twice.

"There's nothing like ripping around on the ice, Kenny," I tell him. He agrees. That night on the broadcast, Ken opens with: "I'm Ken, she's Evanka, and earlier today she played in her very first hockey game and got in a fight!"

I roll my eyes and say, "Yes, and obviously I won the game—and the fight."

Now that I have my first game under my belt, I figure I can only improve from here. And Coach Ethan is hyper-focused on our improvement week to week. He's always reminding us: "Girls, keep your heads up! Keep those legs moving!" If he comes across a great article about women's hockey, he'll tape it to the wall outside our dressing rooms to make sure none of us miss it. "Remember to move your hand down on your stick when you're shooting," he'll say. "Don't grip that stick too tight!"

Coach knows I work in sports—he actually recognized me on the first day of skills, which was a little weird, since hockey and work seem so separate in my mind. Ethan told me he'd been reading a book by John Shannon called *Evolve or Die: Hard-Won Lessons from a Hockey Life*, and wanted to know if I'd read it. I told him I was planning on it but hadn't yet, and then I mentioned I was working on a hockey book myself. "This experience has actually started something for me, in the way of a book," I told him.

"No kidding!" Coach said. After our next skate, he asked me to come into his office and handed me an entire bag of books about hockey. There were so many titles. *Chicken Soup for the Soul: Hooked on Hockey. The Game of Our Lives* by Peter Gzowski. *The Meaning of Puck: How Hockey Explains Modern Canada* by Bruce Dowbiggin. *1972: The Series That Changed Hockey Forever* by Scott Morrison. And, of course, Shannon's book, as we'd discussed.

This gesture was so sweet, but what I immediately noticed is that every book in that bag was written by a man. And that isn't a comment on Coach; it's a comment on what's out there. He also included a USA Hockey Coaching Education Program binder from the program he'd completed back in 2009. Ethan achieved the highest coaching certification level back then and went on to coach AA hockey. He could be coaching a much higher level than us, and he has in the past. He's even coached Denzel Washington's kid. I flip through that binder and it's full of hockey drills I definitely couldn't do. One of the coaching tips is to give players a "compliment sandwich": you point out what an athlete did correctly, point out what was incorrect, and then deliver another compliment. The binder is full of coaching tips like this. Wait: Does Coach Ethan think I have what it takes to become a coach? *What is he trying to tell me?*

I leaf through a bunch of the material, and then ahead of my second-ever scrimmage I pop my head into his office and say: "Thanks for the books, Coach!"

I get dressed for game number two and tell myself I'm going to be a lot more heads-up on the ice than I was last week. We do a few warm-up laps, and then it's game time. I'm breathing hard after my second shift—I'm in no better shape this week than I was last week. Shocking. I squirt water into my mouth while I breathe heavily and check my heart rate: a solid 170. *Whew*. But I might be sweating a little less. Progress.

Robyn gets off the ice shortly after me and sits beside me on the bench, and I look at her and smile while we both breathe hard. Robyn's the one who knows my sister. She's so sweet and kind, and we've talked in the dressing room in the past weeks and recommended books for one another to read. I'm still breathing hard and I'm looking back out on the ice when Robyn turns to me and says: "I heard about your mom, and I'm really sorry."

I was not expecting that—to think about my mum right now—and it's a gut punch. I take a deep breath. "Thank you, Robyn. I appreciate that," I tell her. "It's been tough." My eyes well up with tears, which start to stream down my face as I switch my gaze from her face to the ice. It was such a sweet comment, and so genuine and kind and thoughtful. I know Robyn only meant to acknowledge that my family is going through a difficult time, and I truly do appreciate it. But I wasn't ready for it. It was so out of context, and it snapped me out of my hockey-induced happiness. No one really knows me at hockey on that level yet.

I'm staring at the ice and I will myself to stop crying and then I focus entirely on the puck. The tears dry. I pull myself together, move down the bench so that I'm now closest to the door. A teammate skates off and I get up for my next shift and take the ice and skate as fast as I can. Out on the ice, there's so much happening. I have to concentrate, and I'm thankful for that.

Don't fall, I tell myself. I go through my checklist: *Skate properly.*

Know where the puck is. I'm left wing, so I better stay on the left and try to stay onside. I get the puck and skate up the ice, and a couple of strides later, I pass it to a teammate. She's faster than me and off she goes. I follow her to the net, and she takes a shot, but there's no rebound. About thirty seconds later, I look up at the clock. I'm always very aware of how long I've been on the ice because I don't want to be a hog. Plus, I can't stay out for two minutes—as I learned last week, I get way too gassed. Just over a minute is good, and after the minute's up—I touched the puck and made a pass!—I skate back to the bench and sit down heavily, breathing hard.

I'm smiling again. All my thoughts are focused on my next shift, what I'm hoping to do on the ice.

Hockey has quickly turned into my escape. It's my happy place.

Northern Return

"Guuuuustaaaavo Chaciiiin . . . e."

"Chaseen?"

"Gooose-ta-vo?"

"Chas-en."

"Cha-son?"

I could not, for the life of me, pronounce Gustavo Chacin's name. And that is the reason my boss, Mike English, called me into his office. I knew it, too.

Gustavo was a lefty pitcher from Venezuela, and he had a great rookie season with Toronto back in 2005, with a 13-9 record and a 3.72 ERA in thirty-four starts. Chacin was fifth on the MLB's Rookie of the Year ballots. The 2006 season, though, he struggled and took a step back, and as he got set to make his first few starts of 2007, he was very much in the news as the Blue Jays discussed their plans for him and our analysts got into what the team needed to see from him. That's why I needed to say his name most days, and I could not, for the life of me, do it properly.

"This is a big deal, Evanka," Mike told me, even before I sat down in his office. "You need to get his name right, or your credibility is in question." Mike didn't go so far as to tell me that I'd be fired if I didn't sort this out, but that's definitely how I interpreted our meeting.

Gustavo's last name was tripping me up. And once I messed it up, it was *in my head.* You know how sometimes that can happen, like if you meet someone named Deborah and she says, "I hate being called Debbie" and then you can't help but call her Debbie, or forget if it was Deb or Debbie that she hated? I'd nail the pronunciation of Chacin, and then I'd trip up over which pronunciation it was. I'd repeat "Gustavo Chacin" over and over and over and over (and over) in my head until I got it. And then I'd mess it up and revert back to my mispronunciation. "Chas-en"? No, Evanka. It's "Cha-seen." This was clearly not a smooth start. I'd been on air for three days and I was already in trouble.

Camera operators were correcting me after my hits, which were live, so it was too late. Viewers were ripping me online, and I was trying to stay away from reading the comments posted beneath the clips they'd put on Sportsnet's and Global's websites, but it was impossible not to. "Who's this new girl on Sportsnet? She's not very good," one said. "Does she know what she's talking about?" another said. "She can't read highlights. Does she know sports?" And honestly, it was fair. This was entirely on me, and I was screwing up big-time.

I focused on solving it. I repeated his name over and over and over—the right way. I recorded it and played it back to myself over and over. I wrote it out phonetically and studied it. And then next time I was on air, I nailed it. "Goo-sta-vo Chas-een." Smooth. Perfect. Thank goodness.

"Evanka, you got it!" my producer, Bubba O'Neil, told me after my update on Global that Friday. Darn, it felt good. And once I got it on air, I got it forever. Somehow. *Phew.*

After I got through that self-imposed nightmare in my earliest days at Sportsnet, I honestly was cruising. My second week of work started on the highest note ever, too. On April 9, 2007, Sportsnet sent our whole crew down to the Rogers Centre for the Toronto Blue Jays home opener. (Gustavo Chacin wasn't pitching—but you know I would've been ready if he was!)

We did the show on location, and the on-air broadcast was led by Jamie Campbell.

There Brad and I stood on the field, with second baseman Aaron Hill between us. We asked him about the hopes and expectations for the season. I was absolutely starstruck, smiling from ear to ear while I listened to Aaron give the type of answers you'd expect. "We have a great group," and all that jazz. I wasn't starstruck so much because of Aaron, but realizing this was my job. Wait, I actually get paid for this? I'm on the field? Heck, yeah!

The Jays were playing against the Kansas City Royals. After Brad and I did the pre-game interview with Aaron, I smiled and said: "Thanks for this, Aaron. Back to you, Jamie."

"Thanks, Evanka, great to hear from you," Jamie said. "The Blue Jays are looking to open the season at home with a win . . ."

I could hear Jamie in my earpiece a while longer, and then the sound was cut. There I was, standing on the Rogers Centre turf, grinning, long after my camera was no longer live.

Check me out, doubters, I thought. *I made it!*

Three years ago, I was an engineer.

Two years ago, I was driving thirty-six hours straight to a town I'd never heard of in Arizona to be an anchor on a network I'd never heard of.

A year ago, I was right here interviewing Bengie Molina and introducing myself to Jamie Campbell.

And on this night, Jamie Campbell and I were colleagues on a national broadcast together.

What a trip.

It felt like my career was moving at lightning speed, and that's mainly because I had the perspective of friends and family who were constantly checking in on me and saying, "Sorry, what are you up to now? Didn't you just graduate from engineering? Oh, you're in the desert? Wait, you're on Sportsnet? Evanka? What now? What next?"

I was hitting all the right steps, which felt amazing. And I didn't care to think what was next. This was where I'd wanted to be for a long, long time. I stood on the field and I watched all the fans continue to pour into the Rogers Centre. I stood there for a good long while on that turf, and I thought about how I'd gotten through my first rough patch at work, how I was now here covering the Big Leagues. In broadcasting's big leagues, too.

Oh my gosh, I thought to myself. *Pinch me.*

Last Christmas

It felt nothing like Christmas.

The plan we had, to have a safe-as-possible 2021 COVID Family Christmas at Mum and Tato's, completely fell apart. On Christmas Eve, Kay, her husband, Chris, and their kids, Elizabeth and Jack, all tested positive for COVID. Nothing felt merry.

We'd all been as careful as possible, because we didn't want to compromise Mum's health. We limited our movement and exposure to people. We pulled our kids out of school early. We tested constantly. Nobody said it out loud, but this was our last Christmas with my mum. Our last Christmas together. But Kay and her family were out. Nick's wife, Amy, and their daughter, Lauren, decided to stay home, too, just to be safe.

So it was me, Adam, George, and Blake, my brother Nick, and my parents on Christmas Day. We were trying to make the best of it, but it was so hard. Missing my nieces and nephew made it even tougher, since Christmases lately have always featured little kids running around together, having a blast, being loud, shouting about Santa.

And my mum did everything at Christmas, up until this one.

She'd make the turkey. Decorate the dinner table with garland. Put up the fake Christmas tree, decorate it, and place gifts on the tree skirt for her grandkids. Last Christmas, she bought a drum set for Georgie. The year before that it was a guitar. Jeannie made sure we'd eat around four p.m. so the kids could get to bed at a decent hour at my parents' place—George, Blake, Adam, and I would always stay overnight. The adults, all eight of us, would sit around the big table in the dining room and the kids would eat at a card table beside us. There'd be fresh red poinsettias on both tables. Christmas carols were always playing in the background. It felt festive and joyful.

There was no music playing at our 2021 Christmas, and no flowers to be seen. There were a couple of presents under the fake tree, which was sparsely decorated. No tables were set. Kay made the turkey and potatoes, which we picked up on our way to bring over. Adam and I brought brussels sprouts and salad. Nick brought cookies that Amy made. My mum didn't make anything because she didn't have the strength and energy to even lift her hand, let alone chop something or throw a turkey in the oven.

For our youngest, Blake, who wasn't even two yet, this was his first Christmas with family other than Adam, George, and me. The Christmas before, in 2020, he was nine months old and because of COVID we celebrated over Zoom, as much as you can celebrate on a screen. But 2021 Christmas was somehow even more sad than Christmas on the computer. It wasn't only sad, it was tense. Even George and Blake seemed like toned-down versions of themselves. They wondered where their cousins were. Why Nama wasn't joyful and full of life like she usually was. They knew that she was very sick, because we'd told them, but I think they were still confused.

Mum sat there on the couch, in her spot, hooked up to her

breathing machine. She was attached to that machine nearly all the time at this point. Jeannie's eyes were permanently vacant and lifeless. Her skin looked grey. She got all her nutrition through an IV.

A month before this, in November, she switched from using a cough-assist machine to stir up phlegm and make it easier to breathe and swallow, and now she used this breathing machine all the time. It was hard for her to catch her breath, so she needed the machine to do that for her. Jeannie couldn't lift her arms to hug. She couldn't talk anymore. She couldn't write. Or text. She didn't have the strength to communicate in any way, other than blinking and small smiles.

"Merry Christmas, Mum!" I said, smiling, and I gave her a big hug. Her body felt limp and so, so small. I could feel the bones in her back. "George and Blake made you this card," I told her, and I showed her a card decorated with Batman stickers and random crayon markings, and a pretty good Christmas tree George had drawn on the front. I wrote, "WE LOVE YOU, NAMA! MERRY CHRISTMAS!" on the inside, and the boys coloured all around it. Jeannie smiled when I showed it to her. I put a gift for her under the tree, with no idea whether Tato would open it for her after we'd all gone home. I got her purple pajamas, size extra small because nothing she owns fits anymore. Usually we do a Secret Santa for the adults, but nobody organized that this year. Nobody felt in the spirit, with COVID still rampant, and considering the state of Mum's health.

We always try to limit screen time for George and Blake at home, but this Christmas we were all glued to phones, showing Jeannie what we'd been up to. George skating. Blake tackling George in the snow in our backyard. The boys building a snowman. I knew it would be my last Christmas with my mum, and everyone was on edge for so many reasons. But we tried to bring joy as best as we could. I cried on the drive home that night.

A couple of weeks after that, we celebrated Ukrainian Orthodox Christmas, and it was so much better. It felt like a party. On January 7, which also happens to be my dad's birthday, everyone turned up at my parents' place, having tested negative for COVID. It was a merrier time. Jeannie was still in her spot on the couch, communicating only by way of eye contact. She wore that bright fuchsia sweater she and I bought together on our recent shopping trip. "Merry Christmas, Mum!" I said as I leaned down and wrapped her in a hug. I noticed her hair was matted and messy, so I pulled a comb out of my purse and brushed her hair. I don't think Tato had been brushing it for her, and I understood that, of course. He was doing everything for our mum, and he must have forgotten. I knew it must be exhausting and so sad for him.

We made sure Christmas was as easy as possible: We ordered pierogies and salad and ham and cabbage rolls. Tato picked up kutia—a traditional Ukrainian sweet porridge—from the nearby church. My mum couldn't eat any of it, but the rest of us gathered around the table. The kids ran around together, and the house was loud and felt full. It felt like Christmas should feel.

Nobody said it, but there was a collective understanding that this was probably the last time we'd all be together. Nick captured as many pictures as he could on his phone. "Evanks, you and Mum!" "George, Blake, all the kids, everyone get on the couch with Nama!" He probably took a hundred pictures that night.

"Tato, get on the couch with Mum!" Nick said.

"Happy birthday, Tato," I told my dad after Nick snapped a

dozen photos of him and my mum. As I gave my dad a hug in the kitchen, there were tears in both of our eyes.

Realistically, it made sense to me that this was likely the last time we'd all be together with Jeannie. But it's not something I actually believed. How could there be a day when she wasn't with us?

I tried to focus on the fact that, at this moment, we were all together. I felt sad beyond words, but I had to remember the beauty of the moment.

I don't look back on that Christmas holiday now and remember how my mum couldn't utter a word. How she couldn't move. How she could only sit and watch the grandkids she adored to no end as they zipped around the house, shouting and tackling one another.

We were together, and for that, I am so, so thankful. That's what I'll make sure I remember most.

Impostor Syndrome

The show opened at six p.m. Eastern Time with a montage featuring the big events coming up that night, like a Blue Jays game and a full slate of NHL playoff games. And then out of the commercial break, up flashed the Sportsnet logo, and the focus cut to Brad and me, sitting behind the desk.

"Hi, this is Sportsnet Central with Brad Fay and Evanka Osmak," I'd say. "Brad, what's happening tonight with the Toronto Blue Jays?"

Then off Brad would go, having fun, ad-libbing.

"Glad you asked, Evanka, because there's a big game coming up!"

Meanwhile I sat there, straight-faced and with excellent, robotlike posture, waiting for my next line to appear on the teleprompter. And I'm sure I looked as uncomfortable as I felt.

If you asked my mum, though, I was great. Perfect. But I felt pretty sure Jeannie was the only one who thought that.

If you knew me at all, and you saw me on TV, you'd see it for yourself: I was awfully stiff. "Do you have to sit up so straight, so rigidly?" my friend Lara asked. And as many questions as my brother, Nick, had asked about how awesome my job was, he also wondered: "You're doing great, but is everything you say scripted? Can you work in any of your own personality, or is that frowned upon?" I know Nick wasn't asking those questions unkindly. But adding personality only increased the likelihood I'd say something stupid, right?

Despite my obvious discomfort with the on-air part of my job, it actually felt like I was surrounded by absolute awesomeness. Honestly, I wondered how on earth I'd landed this gig. I'd come into work at two p.m. to prepare for the six o'clock Ontario show, and I'd get my hair and makeup done. Brad and I were on the air from six to seven p.m., and then I was done for the day. I earned more money than I did as an engineer. It was honestly unreal.

When I started in 2007, it was the heyday of highlight shows. Sportsnet had a full slate—seven highlight shows in all, every night and into the early morning, and from three different time zones. Brad and I were the six p.m. Eastern show. There were also six p.m. shows in the Mountain and Pacific time zones. And ten p.m. shows in each region, plus a morning show from Ontario that aired across the country. All seven shows had different hosts, making for a busy newsroom. None of us were aware of how much our industry would change in the coming years. I did one hour-long show in the early stages of my career, and later on, I'd do four shows a night, for different time zones across the country.

Since Brad and I were the earliest on air, we usually teed up the next sports events, with a focus on the NHL and Blue Jays games. The communications giant, Rogers, which currently owns Sportsnet, also owns 80 per cent of the Toronto Blue Jays, and has the rights to televise all 162 Jays games every season. On nights there were Jays games, Brad and I were only on the air for half an hour because of the pre-game baseball show that started at six thirty. Sometimes we'd have highlights from soccer games that aired earlier in the day, or the odd tennis match, or the opening round of a PGA golf tournament on a Thursday or Friday. But usually Brad and I were looking ahead. We wrote up a lot of previews every night, and a producer decided which stories went where, and assigned on-cameras to Brad or me.

Brad was incredibly kind, but we didn't have a ton in common. We were in very different phases of our lives: He was married with kids, and more than fifteen years older than me. I felt intimidated by Brad, though that was no fault of his. It's just that everything still felt new and intimidating to me. I was so focused on not screwing up that I couldn't feel like myself. I was just trying to get through the show without making a mistake.

"The Blue Jays take on the Boston Red Sox tonight," I said, looking into the camera, and then we showed a clip of pitcher Roy Halladay warming up, followed by Blue Jays manager John Gibbons chiming in on how reliable the righty "Doc" had been in the lineup. In his start before this one, Doc had pitched a complete ten-inning win, and he was one of the best pitchers in baseball. I was on camera for maybe twenty seconds during this clip, and I'd written my script in a very straightforward way, with no embellishments. "Halladay has a 2.35 ERA and he's looking to earn his third straight win on the mound," I said, reading directly from the teleprompter, sitting in my chair stiff as a board. I didn't say anything about how incredible Halladay's season was, I didn't look at Brad with wide eyes and comment on how clutch the righty had been for his team, like I would if I felt at all confident, or like myself. Like the way I talked to Lara about baseball. I couldn't do that on air. I knew what a great opportunity this was, I knew it was my dream job, but I was having trouble finding my own voice.

Brad picked up my last mention of Doc—"The Red Sox might want to call a doctor after this one, if Halladay's start this season is any indication," he said, grinning—and then he seamlessly launched into introducing a first-round NHL playoff game that night between the Vancouver Canucks and the Dallas Stars. I just sat there, focused on what I had to say next.

Looking back on it, I wonder how much of the pressure I felt to be perfect was because I was one of the few women on air. There were just three women on camera in the Toronto studio in 2007. It was me, Martine Gaillard (the star anchor in our market), and Daru Dhillon, who did two-minute segments about quirky happenings in the sports world.

"I'm so scared to mess up," I told Martine one afternoon while we were in the office together. She told me she understood the feeling completely. "Just remember: You know your stuff," she said. "You deserve to be here." It felt so nice to have a teammate like Martine.

A couple of months into my time at Sportsnet, all the anchors were called in for photo shoots for promotional material. Some of the pictures would be on billboards and on signs on the TTC—our public transit system in Toronto. But you wouldn't see my face there. The big promotions were for Martine and Sean McCormick, the top anchor duo in Ontario, who did the local ten p.m. show. The idea of being promoted by Sportsnet in any way did excite me, though, so I went to the photo shoot feeling pretty jazzed. As for what I'd wear, I had been shopping with a clothing consultant shortly after I started, and we'd picked out a bright red leather blazer—high collar, button-down, and long, with pockets on the boobs. I found absolutely nothing about it appealing: the length, the boob pockets, and the bright colour, since I prefer black. But I know colours pop on TV, and the clothing consultant, Linda, absolutely loved the jacket on me. "You should wear it for the photo shoot," she told me. "Okay, let's do it!" I said. But honestly, I really disliked the jacket, and it wasn't me at all. Since I had no idea what I was doing, I went with whatever Linda said.

A few days after the shoot, photos of the anchors appeared on the website. Everyone else looked great, glitzy and glamorous. If you asked me, I looked *terrible*. And it made me feel pretty terrible, too. I felt like I didn't belong among all those dazzling, shiny anchors.

One of the other reasons my outfit bothered me so much is that, truthfully, appearance consumes too much of my brain. I know this, and it has been a problem since I was a teenager. And since I put myself out there on TV every night—in the age of social media, now, too—you can probably imagine the feedback I sometimes get from total strangers about my looks. People comment when I cut my hair two inches shorter. I swear they notice more often than my husband does. I can laugh some of it off, but honestly, I know that my bottom teeth are crooked and I want to fix them, but I don't need strangers reminding me my teeth aren't straight.

Being on TV and having my appearance scrutinized by viewers who've never met me is one of the most difficult parts of the job for me, even after fifteen years at Sportsnet. It's hard when people point out deficiencies and you already see them yourself.

I work hard to look and feel as good as I can. I exercise every single day. I watch what I eat.

I feel pressure to look my best on television because the reality of my job at Sportsnet is that looks really do matter. Or rather, appearance matters. That is something I understand and I do appreciate, because when I watch TV, I want to see people dressed nicely, or maybe wearing something I would wear.

That's probably also why that red leather blazer I wore during my first promo shoot bothered me so much. It definitely wasn't something I would usually wear. But I had to try to get over it. It was done. So I didn't look at my photo on the website very often.

And lucky for me, my pictures were only online. Martine in her beautiful green suit jacket and amazing blond hair and Sean in his sharp white button-up were on billboards around the city.

And while in many ways I felt like I didn't quite belong on air when I first started working, I found my stride off the air pretty quickly. So much of that was thanks to Martine, because we became good friends. With Martine, it was easygoing and fun, and there was a feeling of women supporting one another, since we were few and far between. "I wonder if it's a Canadian thing, if Canadians are just kinder in the industry," I told my mum over the phone, about a month into my time at Sportsnet. We chatted almost every day about work and life, Jeannie and me.

Our chats had to be over the phone soon after I started the new gig. I moved into a one-bedroom apartment in downtown Toronto, at King and Simcoe, about three months into my contract. I figured it was time—I was twenty-seven, after all. "I thought you were great last night!" Mum told me one morning while we were catching up. "I love that blue blouse you had on. Where is it from?"

Mum was so happy she could watch me regularly on TV. She'd been around sports for decades as a spectator, but now she had a reason to watch the pre-game shows, which she never had an interest in before. She never missed a show, and she actually retained facts about sports. "The Blue Jays are on a roll," she told me. Look at you go, sports fan Jeannie! She even gave up her worn-out Rita MacNeil CD in the car and started listening exclusively to Sportsnet 590 The Fan on the radio instead. She didn't want to miss it if I was on, and she also wanted to keep up with what was going on in sports so we could talk about it later.

But most of Mum's questions in my earliest days at Sportsnet were about friends I'd made there. Jeannie was so happy to hear that I was getting close to some of my colleagues.

In the summer of 2007, Martine and I started hanging out a lot, and it was easy, since we both worked evenings. She invited me out with some of her other friends in broadcasting, like Robin Gill, who was working in news at a big station, Global. We'd go out late, since we all worked evenings. It was awesome. Most of the girls I met in the industry were a couple years older than me, and we were all single and wanting to have a good time. It was so nice for me, especially since I'd moved back to Toronto to find that Lara and most of my other friends had serious boyfriends or fiancés they were living with. Now I also had another crew of fun, smart, awesome women to hang out with on a nightly basis, who had the same lifestyle as I did.

It made me rethink my timeline on what I needed in life. It made me feel young! There was no rush to settle down with some guy, or to start having kids (I didn't want them, anyway). This was the time to have fun! We went to fancy restaurants, and we all lived and worked downtown. It was that sweet spot in life where you're independent, you're young, and you can focus on fun. It was great being around older people in the industry who were established, who were celebrities, but who weren't catty. They made me feel comfortable.

I gravitated toward the other women, and found they were all so supportive. We asked one another questions, related our experiences. Our in-studio female crew at Sportsnet was also supportive: We had each other's backs, we cheered each other on. It was such a motivating and wonderful group to be a part of. Even if my on-air role kept changing.

About six months into my time at Sportsnet, in the late fall of 2007, I got called into Mike English's office again. "We're moving you to the morning show," he told me. This was amazing news, if you asked me. The morning show taped in the same spot, at Agincourt in Scarborough, about a half-hour drive from my apartment in Toronto. Since I'd start the show once the games were over for the night, around one a.m., the hours weren't great for my social life, so I had to say goodbye to regular dinners and dates with my friends. But I saw it as a great step in my career; I'd have my own show with no co-anchor, and it was so fun to read highlights. It was a big change, and I saw it as a promotion, since it meant the network trusted me to be on my own for an entire show. I was also excited to fine-tune my skills reading and writing highlights.

I'd get to the office around nine p.m. to write and prepare, and during NHL playoffs, with a series like Vancouver against Dallas going to quadruple overtime, some nights I'd drive home at five-thirty in the morning. Thank goodness I didn't have to wake up early the next day. And somehow I didn't feel tired in those days. I felt energized because I loved my work and I loved my life. And heck, I was in my twenties with boundless energy. Oh, if only I still felt that way . . .

I was on that early-morning show for about a year. Then Mike told me he was moving me to the weekend show, with an established anchor on our network, Jim Lang. We'd do three shows on Saturdays and three on Sundays, at six p.m., ten p.m., and also the morning show, which taped at one a.m., or whenever games ended on the West Coast.

I really felt like I was getting the hang of the one a.m. show, but the nerves kicked in again with the change to the weekend shows. Being paired with an established anchor like Jim was exciting, but also scary. I was still scared of being wrong, which I figured would end up getting me fired, and that fear was magnified alongside a more experienced anchor. Any mistake I made would have any naysayers claiming, "I told you she couldn't do this job!" I spiraled easily to the worst-case scenario.

Three years into my time at Sportsnet, I was still trying to find my voice. When we had staff meetings, I didn't speak up much. I think it was in part because I was always one of the few women in the room, sometimes the only woman, along with about ten men. I was also managing the fact that I'm quiet, I put lots of pressure on myself, I wanted to please everyone, and I didn't want to mess up. Wouldn't that get me fired?

As I prepared to get to work on my third show in as many years at Sportsnet with an established anchor partner in Jim Lang, I wondered if I'd ever really feel like myself on camera.

The End

George had to miss school, Blake couldn't go to day care, and I couldn't go to work. So Adam, George, Blake, and I packed up and headed to our family cottage in Muskoka. We didn't know what else to do, and we knew we couldn't be around other people.

It was January of 2022, and Adam had come home from a ski trip with buddies and tested positive for COVID. I had to email my boss to tell him I wouldn't be available for at least a few days. So we headed up north to isolate together and hope for the best. It was the first time any of us tested positive, and we figured we were all in it together.

My mum's seventy-third birthday was three days away, on January 23. And she was lying in a bed in an emergency ward at Oakville Trafalgar Memorial Hospital, struggling to breathe.

This was the second time Jeannie looked at my dad and either choked out, "Can't breathe," or tried to write, "Can't breathe" unsuccessfully because she didn't have the strength to hold a pen. She managed to choke out the word "am-bu-lance" this time, so my dad called one. Mum had already been to the hospital once, about a week before. But this time, the doctor told us it wasn't looking good for her long-term, that this might be it. Jeannie then sent a text to Nick, Kay, and me. It read: "I love you all so much. I hope you know that. I hope you remember it forever." I couldn't imagine how much time it took her to type that out herself, given she barely had the strength to lift the phone. Maybe my dad wrote it. It felt so uncomfortable. And heartbreaking. I'd never received a message from someone who knew they were about to die. My mum had realized that she was coming to the end. That this was it.

On our way up to the cottage, I had been on the phone for most of the two-hour drive with either my dad or Nick or Kay, talking about next steps for my mum as far as her care went. It was clear she needed more support. We didn't all agree about what was best for Jeannie, though. "We can't put her in a home," I told my dad. I was pushing instead for a caregiver in their home in Oakville. "COVID is so bad right now! What do you think will happen to her in a home?" I asked.

For the last week, this is all we'd been talking about, Tato and Kay and Nick and me. Ever since my mum first had to go to the hospital in early January of 2022, we knew we had to do something to provide her with more care, and it was so stressful for my family, because nobody knew for sure what was best for her. Adam has some connections in the healthcare industry through work, so I told my family I'd look into services and explore the possibilities there.

When Adam, George, Blake, and I arrived at the cottage, we got settled and immediately got the fire going. We played board games. We looked out at the partially frozen lake. We drank hot chocolate. We had fun, but I truly couldn't enjoy anything. My mind was consumed with what we were going to do to ensure Jeannie was as comfortable as possible. "She can't keep asking for ambulances," I told Adam through tears after dinner, after we'd put the boys to bed.

Then, on January 23, we FaceTimed my dad and asked him to put the phone up to my mum. She was lying in her hospital bed with a ventilator on her face. "Happy birthday to you, happy birthday to you!" Adam, George, and I sang. George really held the "youuuuuu!" and belted out that birthday tune at the top of his lungs, holding his arms out wide. Blake, who was nearly two, stared into the iPad and tried to hit buttons with his chubby bear-paw hands. "Happy birthday to Nama, happy birthday to youuuuuuuu!"

We were all cheering and Blake started clapping, and we were looking at my mum, who was just lying there in her hospital bed. I couldn't tell if she was smiling underneath all those tubes, but I hoped she was. I couldn't tell if she could hear us. I knew if she could, she'd probably be smiling, just at the sight of the kids. It was her seventy-third birthday, and she spent it in the emergency room. After three days at the hospital, she still didn't have a room at Oakville Trafalgar.

"We love you so much," I said into the iPad, and then we all said goodbye. I texted Tato that I'd be sending updates on some private home care options I'd found, and he sent a thumbs-up back.

The day after Mum's birthday seemed long. We spent most of it outside playing with George and Blake, walking around in the snow, making little tobogganing hills, making snow angels, trying to enjoy winter up north. At night after dinner, we got together around the table and did a giant puzzle that featured trees and animals and outdoor scenes.

On January 25, I woke up at four a.m.—I hadn't been able to sleep longer than four or five hours at a time that whole week because my mind was constantly racing. And once I was awake on that particular morning, I knew exactly what I needed to do when the day actually got started. As soon as Adam woke up at the more reasonable time of seven a.m., I told him: "I need to get home." Adam was still the only member of our family who had tested positive for COVID.

I packed up George and Blake and we started driving back to Oakville after lunch. Adam was staying at the cottage to take a couple of meetings, and he'd drive home later that night. Both boys snoozed during our drive, and I could hear them getting sick—their breathing sounded laboured. I called my mother-in-law, Lindsay, to let her know we were coming home, and she said she'd drop off some medication for the kids at our place.

Then I called Lara. She'd moved to LA to work as a showrunner and writer, and she'd been with me every step of the way when it came to my mum. "We're trying to figure out what to do next," I told her.

"Evanka, I'm so sorry," Lara said. "Please keep me posted on how she's doing. Call me any time. I'm here for you."

She knew Jeannie well, had known my mum since we were ten-year-old kids, the only girls who tried out for the Appleby boys' soccer team.

I put Blake to bed just before six p.m. because he was exhausted after only having a short nap in the car. George and I watched TV while I emailed my family about the private-care options I'd found for Mum. I was hoping we'd go this direction, and I think Kay agreed with me. Nick and Tato wondered if a home would be a better bet for Mum, so she'd be closer to more medical care than a home healthcare professional could provide. At this point we were all so frustrated with the fact she was still in the emergency room at the hospital. Only one of us could visit her at a time because of COVID, so we needed to make a decision as soon as possible, to get her out of there.

My phone rang just after seven p.m. It was Tato.

"Evanks, your mum just went into cardiac arrest," he told me calmly. "Can you get here as soon as you can?"

"Yes, of course," I said, and we hung up.

I didn't even give myself time to register what that meant. Cardiac arrest.

"George, we've got to go to Oakville," I told him, turning off the TV. I immediately launched into emergency and panic mode. "Let's get your shoes on, okay, buddy? We've got to go see Nama. She's not okay."

George looked at me, but he didn't follow me toward the front door. "But what about Blake?" he asked.

"Oh my gosh," I said, wide-eyed.

My four-year-old had the presence of mind to remember we'd be leaving a sleeping eighteen-month-old at home, and I did not.

"Thank you, Georgie," I said, and there were tears in my eyes as he leaned in to give me a hug. I picked up my cell again and called my in-laws. My mother-in-law said she'd be over right away, since they live around the corner. I waited at the door with my purse and I ran outside when I saw a car parking in our driveway. It was my brother-in-law, Henry.

George overheard me tell Henry that my mum "isn't doing well" and George walked over and wrapped me in another hug, the biggest one his little arms could muster. It was like my five-year-old could sense I needed a hug. I squeezed him so tight. Then George and Henry headed inside so I could get into the car and drive to the hospital on my own.

I immediately dialled Adam from the car to tell him to drive home, and luckily he was already on his way. We met at Yorkdale Mall, and I left my car there and hopped into his. His right arm was around me as we drove the rest of the way to the hospital. We were flying across the 401 when my text alarm chimed. It was my sister.

"She's gone."

No.

No. No!

This couldn't be true.

I broke down and sobbed uncontrollably. Tears, snot, saliva, everything, everywhere. My mind was racing.

My mum couldn't be gone. That couldn't be true. I felt guilt and sadness and anger all at once.

"I never got to say goodbye!" I said as I cried in the car. Adam was doing his best to comfort me while he drove. I cried for the rest of the ten-minute drive to the hospital. "You go home and be with the kids," I told Adam, and then I walked into Oakville Trafalgar while I wiped tears from my face.

I found my mum's room and saw Tato and Nick and Kay first, all crying, standing around her bed. My mum was still lying there, but it didn't look like her. I reached out to touch her hand, but it didn't feel like her. Jeannie's skin was a colour I can't describe. She looked empty. She felt and looked like someone I didn't know, not the woman who raised me, the woman I'd loved my whole life. It was beyond awful to see her like this, so unlike herself. Like a stranger. I couldn't bear it.

"I love you, Mum," I told her while tears streamed down my cheeks. "I'm so sorry I wasn't here in time to say goodbye."

Tato, Kay, Nick, and I were all standing around her, hugging, looking at each other, often in silence. After fifteen minutes or so, we wondered: *What do we do now?*

"I love you," I told my mum once more, and I picked up her hand one last time before we walked out of the emergency room.

I got in Tato's car and we drove back to the house my dad now lived in alone, and Nick and Kay drove there in Kay's car. From the car, Tato called my mum's brother, Bill. The conversation was short and my dad didn't cry. Maybe he was in shock. As he drove I texted Lara: "She's gone." I didn't look to see her response, but she must've been shocked, too. Only a few hours earlier we were talking about next steps for my mum's care, and now she was dead.

We arrived at my parents' house. We managed small smiles as we poured four glasses of Johnnie Walker Black Label scotch. "To Jeannie," my dad said, and we all said, "Cheers" and sipped scotch in honour of my mum, who loved Johnnie Black. Scotch tastes disgusting, if you ask me, and Kay and I choked down our sips. I think Mum would've been proud.

Tato was in disbelief; we all were. It was too early to accept this. It didn't seem possible that we left the hospital without her and we would never get her back. That hadn't registered. It couldn't register.

As we sat around in the family room, Tato started to tell stories. "That night we met in Windsor," he said, smiling, as he remembered seeing my mum for the first time, "I'll never forget hearing her laugh when I told her I'd crashed the wedding."

"Wait—what?" Nick said.

"Tato, you never told us you crashed the wedding!" I said.

Then we started laughing. We'd heard parts of this story before, and knew that my dad, who's a few years older than my mum, had met her at a wedding. Except we never knew he'd crashed it!

"No way, Tato," I told him, eyebrows way up, a huge grin on my face.

"Who do you think you are, Vince Vaughn?" Nick asked, laughing, referencing that classic movie, *Wedding Crashers*.

My dad filled in more of the details, that my mum was sixteen years old and living in Windsor, Ontario, where her aunt Dolly lived. Since both of my parents were Ukrainian, they knew a bunch of the same people, and my mum was a bridesmaid in her friend's wedding. "We knew the couple well enough," Tato told us, of himself and a couple of buddies who showed up at the reception uninvited.

"I asked your mum out on a date that night," he said, smiling.

We know the other details well: that Borden and Jeannie had gone to a festival together a few days later. Tato never said he knew from that moment that my mum was the woman he wanted to be with forever. He's not mushy like that. But his watering eyes as he recounted how they met told us everything he wouldn't gush about: She'd been his partner for life, and he was so thankful. As hard as it was to say goodbye, as hard as it had been to see her at her worst, he and my mum had lived a beautiful life together, and all because Tato had pulled a *Wedding Crashers* move and showed up uninvited to that wedding.

"To be a fly on the wall that night," Kay said, smiling.

"What did her dress look like?" I asked.

"You think I remember?" he said, laughing. "That was more than fifty years ago, Evanks!"

My parents were married for more than half a century.

The four of us kept talking, laughing, and crying for a few more hours. Kay and I switched to water, while Tato and Nick stuck with Jeannie's favourite scotch.

Then we headed home. As we drove, I thought about the last time I saw my mum. It was a week earlier, on one of my regular visits. When I'd said, "Bye, Mum, I love you," I didn't think it would be the last time she'd ever hear me say those words. I didn't think it would be the last time I'd ever get a chance to say that to her while she was still here.

I could not believe I didn't get to say goodbye one last time. I felt guilty. I felt awful. I felt empty.

New Beginnings

I was very aware of a trend when it came to my time at Sportsnet. It was 2010, and ever since I had started working the desk with a co-anchor more than a year earlier, nobody had lasted in the role sitting beside me for longer than a few months. Four months, for those keeping count. I know I was.

"But you're still there, Evanka—what does that tell you?" Mum asked me one afternoon during one of our daily phone chats. "It means you're great!"

Thanks for your entirely unbiased and perfectly objective opinion, Jeannie.

It really hurt to see my colleagues let go. I was especially sad when I heard Sportsnet was cutting ties with Jim Lang. He and I got along great. He was a lot of fun, super welcoming, and it was easy to come to work and sit beside him on the desk. Jim loves the Canadian Football League and the National Football League, and he especially loves his Oakland Raiders.

Jim and I had become friends, but we didn't hang out in our spare time. Like my first co-anchor, Brad, we were at such different stages in our lives. Jim has a couple of daughters who are into various activities, and he's a good decade older than me. I was twenty-eight and living it up, spending my evenings having fun with friends. I had been dating casually for a while, not taking anyone too seriously, but had just started seeing this guy Adam that I'd met at the 2010 Olympics.

It wasn't a totally random run-in with Adam—there was a backstory to meeting him in person. My girlfriend Jess from Queen's had told me about him, saying, "You have to meet Adam! I think you two would really hit it off." She'd told him the same about me. Jess loves matchmaking, but she had never actually put us in touch.

Still, we did meet, about a month later. I was in Vancouver covering the 2010 Winter Olympics, and I was with my girlfriend Elizabeth at the Canada Hockey House. It was a space designed specifically for Team Canada, where hockey played on TVs basically 24/7, and it was a real party atmosphere. We were there watching the Canada-Russia quarterfinal men's hockey game, and the Hockey House was raucous. Lots of cheering, lots of cheers-ing. Canada was in the midst of a blowout that would end with a 7–3 win. During the drubbing, before Corey Perry scored two goals for Canada, a tall guy with dark hair and a beer in his hand walked over and said: "Evanka! I'm Adam. Our mutual friend Jess said we should meet."

So this was the guy Jess had been telling me about.

I later found out that Adam had texted Jess minutes earlier to let her know I had turned up there—he'd recognized me from TV. "Go on over and introduce yourself, Casanova!" she'd written back. And so Adam had. He was there with his cousins, and they were obviously a few beers deep: red-cheeked, chatty, a touch wobbly. Adam and I talked for a while, and then we said goodbye.

After the game was over, around seven p.m., Elizabeth and I

were walking past a McDonald's on the way back to my hotel and I heard "Evanka!" It was Adam again, Big Mac in hand. "I've got an extra ticket for the Slovakia-Finland quarterfinal game tonight. Do you want to come?"

"No, but thanks for the offer," I told him. "I have to be up early for my shift tomorrow."

"Oh," Adam said. "Okay."

I found out later that his cousins were *really* razzing him about that. "You can't even get the sports girl to go to a hockey game with you?" they said, laughing.

Adam was thinking that himself, but before we said goodbye, we exchanged phone numbers (that was my idea, because I'm super suave). So I think he believed me that I had to be in bed early for my shift the next day. It was the truth. This guy was super nice, funny, smart, and handsome, but my alarm was going off at five a.m. Early bedtime was key.

Part of the reason I wanted a good rest is that I felt a lot of pressure during these Olympic shifts. I'd studied for months in advance, but still, there were so many sports, so many athletes, so much to be on top of. Looking back, I underestimated it all. And since I was worried about my performance, I'd go online to see what viewers thought about me, and I'd read way too many comments. "She doesn't know what she's talking about" was the common refrain. And: "Who's this girl, anyway?" It was a bigger audience watching me than I was used to, and they weren't fans. My self-confidence was the lowest it had been in years.

Learning the ins and outs of the biathlon and educating myself on all of Canada's medal hopefuls at a home Games was a massive job. I was consumed with trying to do my best.

Adam and I texted back and forth during the rest of the Olympics, but didn't see each other again in Vancouver. I was too busy, honestly. But we did make a plan to get together for St. Patrick's Day back in Toronto. A date.

When St. Paddy's Day rolled around, Adam said he'd pick me up. I agreed to that, since Jess knew him, and surely she'd tell me if he was a serial killer, right? He came by my place, and I was armed with a couple of pens and two NCAA March Madness brackets that I'd printed out. I figured we could fill those out if we didn't have anything to talk about. I like to be prepared, okay? And I'd been on enough dates to know if this was a disaster, I needed a backup plan to keep us entertained. I figured we could discuss the merits of picking Duke to win it all if we found ourselves lacking in conversation. I couldn't exactly just check out early, since we had a mutual friend, and I didn't want to be a jerk if this date was a total bust.

We went out for dinner in the east end of Toronto. I pulled those brackets out of my purse just after we sat down and Adam laughed at me. Well, we spent the whole dinner talking. Not long after that, we started dating.

It was so nice to have someone steady in my life, someone I was falling in love with, someone I wanted to be around all the time.

I had Adam. I had great pals outside of work. I had great pals at work, like Martine. The only thing in my life that wasn't steady, to be honest, was my co-anchor on the desk. That was a revolving door. It's the nature of our industry. Journalism can be tough to get into, and tough to stick with, as I'd learned in my short career so far.

Still I couldn't help but wonder if there was something I was doing wrong. Something about me that made it difficult for my co-anchor to connect with. I questioned whether I could have done something different to keep my last co-anchor, Jim, in the chair beside me.

It didn't help that when people found out what I did for work, the question I'd get most often was: "But . . . do you actually like sports?" It made me doubt whether I was good enough. It also made me wonder: Would they be asking me that question if I was a man?

Probably not.

The co-anchor beside me kept changing and then, in the spring of 2011, Sportsnet hired a guy named Ken Reid. I knew nothing about him other than the fact that he'd worked at our competitor, TSN. He came in for the first time on a Saturday, ahead of our six p.m. show. A producer introduced us: "Ken, this is Evanka. Evanka, meet Ken."

Ken and I said hi at the same time and stuck out our hands for a shake.

And I'm sure at this moment, everyone at the station was thinking: "Good luck! You won't last long. Maybe you can do something different than all the other guys and somehow manage to hang around?"

Well, that's definitely what I was thinking: Here we go again, my fourth co-anchor in less than four years. The Great Search for Evanka Osmak's Co-Anchor resumes.

I gave this new guy six months, tops, before Sportsnet decided he wasn't the right fit. And hey, that would be a record for me.

Aftermath

|woke up at four a.m. and my mind was racing. I couldn't sleep. My body hurt from heaving and weeping, from this full-body sadness I didn't know a person could feel. It was January 26, 2022, and it had been fewer than twelve hours since my mum died. I was nowhere near believing it. I couldn't breathe, thinking about it. She couldn't be gone.

But my denial wasn't working. Jeannie was dead. Later that morning, I took another COVID test. It was positive, and I felt numb about it. I didn't think I could possibly feel worse. I had been staying away from my mum in what would prove to be her final days because Adam had tested positive, and I figured I'd catch it. But I hadn't, until after she was gone. And so I missed seeing her in her final moments because I was being overly cautious.

This positive test meant I couldn't be around my dad, sister, and brother when they needed me. I could only help with things like funeral planning over the phone. I couldn't wrap my dad or my sister or my brother in a giant hug. We couldn't sob together in person. In between bouts of tears that seemed like they'd never stop, I spent the first day without my mum calling people she loved and who loved her to let them know she was gone.

I called the parents of my friend Ainsley. I called up our family friend Maggie, and she told me to pass onto my dad that she was so sorry, and she'd be there if he needed her. I called up a whole bunch of my friends and Jeannie's friends to let them know, and I repeated the same sentiments over and over. "She's gone. We all love and miss her so much. She loved you dearly. Thank you for your support." Everybody cried; I felt like I couldn't stop crying.

Lara and I had the longest conversation about my mum, and when I hung up, I was an absolute basket case. I couldn't repeat the details again. I couldn't talk about Mum anymore. I was spent. I texted Ken and his wife to let them know. My phone rang a few minutes later and it was Kenny, but I couldn't pick up. I couldn't go through it all again. I knew he'd understand.

I felt a type of pain I'd never experienced, both emotionally and physically. My body ached from the depths the pain was coming from. My gut felt like it was bruised on the inside. This must be what absolute grief feels like.

Adam and the kids went back to the cottage to give me a chance to grieve by myself. I didn't want Georgie and Blake to see me so shattered, and I figured I needed to be alone to feel everything I was feeling. As much as I wanted the joy of being around the boys, it was nice that they weren't home so I could be as sad as I felt. I just wanted to sit in the hurt and feel it.

The sleeping pills I took weren't working. I ate, but not much. I broke down sobbing all the time, and when I breathed deeply at the end of a cry, I felt a sense of relief that only lasted a few moments until I was crying again. Grief, I realized, is such a lonely thing. Everyone who knew and loved my mum were all going through it, but it felt lonely anyway. We were all left to deal with it as best we could, and everybody was coping differently. I couldn't imagine what it must have been like for my dad. Just the thought of him alone in my parents' house made me sob and heave and double over.

Flowers and lasagnes were being delivered to our house and to my dad's and brother's and sister's, and we were overwhelmed with the generosity and support and kindness of the many people who loved my mum. I went back and forth between feeling the lowest of lows and being so grateful for the many wonderful people in our lives. Being grateful for the fact my mum had so many people who cared about her. I also felt useless since I couldn't visit funeral homes while I had COVID or help my family prepare for Jeannie's funeral. I was alone with my feelings, and maybe that was a good thing. I didn't want anyone seeing me like this.

I leaned a lot on my friend Christine, who called me up two days after Jeannie's passing. I answered and burst into tears instead of saying, "Hello." Christine had lost her dad two months earlier. She remembered the heaving and the crying and feeling like she'd never recover. "Evanka, I know you can't tell right now, but you're going to get through it," she told me. "I think you'll always feel the loss. I still cry about my dad almost every day, and I know I'll miss him forever. But you get to the other side and you can be yourself again. I promise."

Those were the most promising words I'd heard since Jeannie died, and I told Christine I'd try to believe her. I've known her since high school—we'd met at a graduation formal, and then ran into each other at Queen's, where we were also roommates. She was an incredible source of support when I needed it most.

"Evanka, call me any time you want to talk, okay?" she said. "I'm always here for you. I'm planning a girls' trip for this summer, and I'll fill you in on the details. You need to be there."

Christine didn't ask if I wanted to come on the trip. She knew I needed to come on the trip.

I told Christine: "I'll be there." And I think I meant it.

Girlfriends are the best.

A few days later, I tested negative for COVID. I could drive around with my dad to look at cemetery plots, and give him the hug I'd been wanting to give him for days. Cry on his shoulder. Give him a chance to cry on mine, though he didn't take me up on that. Tato was holding it together, but he looked worn out, as tired as I'd ever seen him. When we hugged, I held on to him for a long time.

Tato and I talked about Jeannie's fun, easy laugh that got everyone else laughing. It made both of us smile.

Our family decided we'd have a small funeral with just twelve of us, on a Monday, since COVID was still rampant. In the summertime, we'd have a party in my parents' backyard when Jeannie's garden was blooming and beautiful, and we could have more people around to celebrate her the way she deserved to be celebrated, around her beautiful hydrangeas.

For the small family funeral, Kay and I picked out a black dress with long sleeves, pearl earrings, and a pearl necklace for our mum to wear. Mum loved her pearls. We buried her with her wedding rings. With makeup on, Jeannie looked like herself again. Her grandkids made cards that we put in an envelope in her casket. George's had a picture of an airplane on it, and it read: "Nama, I love you forever!" I felt that heave of emotion when I saw his card.

My mum wasn't going to see my boys, and all her grandkids, grow up. I couldn't take it, so I pretended it wasn't true. That was the only way I could cope.

The day we said goodbye to my mum was cold: February 1, 2022. A priest was present, and while we barely knew him, it was nice to have someone around who was so well-versed in awkward conversations around grief, when everyone else is so distraught. That's a skill of its own. As I watched her coffin descend into the ground, I felt awful and surreal and weird, but having the kids running around was comforting; they were so young they didn't understand what it meant. I needed that distraction.

It made me so sad to think that Blake and Georgie didn't have their Nama anymore, and I didn't have my mum. But as I looked at Blake and George dressed up in their little suits, I also thought to myself: *I'm so grateful for these two*. I hoped I could have a positive impact on my own kids the way my mum did on me. Now that I'm a parent, I have a greater appreciation for my mum and all the work she did to keep our family organized and fed and clean and happy, work that was too often unnoticed. I feel such gratitude for my mum, and I can't help thinking that I want my kids to feel about me the way I felt about Jeannie. Thankful and so happy I had a mum like her.

As I've said, there was a time when I really didn't want kids, and Jeannie knew it. Maybe she always thought I'd come around, or maybe she wasn't convinced, I'll never know. But I'll never forget when Adam and I called up my parents back in 2016 to tell them we were expecting for the first time, and my mum screamed into the phone. I think she was in shock. That was fair, because I'd done a one-eighty at thirty-five and changed my mind about kids. Adam was so excited, because I think deep down, he'd always wanted kids.

"Evanks, Adam, we can't wait to meet this little one!" Mum shouted.

She only got to know George for four years, and Blake for just under two. But we're all so grateful for that time.

When I got home from the funeral, I booked a trip to go see Lara in LA two days later. She had called and said I needed to come visit her, and I agreed. I could stay with her family, her husband and their three daughters.

When I arrived in LA, Lara and I were both crying as we hugged. We laughed, we talked, we cried some more. It was exactly what I needed, a visit with my best friend, who knew my mum so well. "You're so much like her, you know that?" Lara told me.

She'd been in LA for four years, and I hadn't visited her until now. I hated that it took something so devastating to get me out there to see my best friend. We were both busy with life and young children, but it was no excuse. I promised myself and Lara that I'd be back soon.

We FaceTimed Lara's mom, Therese, who lived in Malta, and we all cried. Therese and Jeannie were good friends, and they met through us kids. "Her laugh!" Therese said, tearing up. "Nobody laughed like your mum. She was so much fun. She was always the first to appreciate my bad jokes." Lara remembered when my mum took her, Ainsley, and me to Hilton Head in South Carolina while we were in high school. "Best March break ever!" Lara said. "We had the time of our lives." Jeannie had gone to Lara's wedding. Our families were that close.

I headed home after three days of laughing and crying in LA

with Lara. I hugged her so tight before I got in my Uber and crawled through LA traffic to get to the airport. I knew I'd only just waded into grieving my mum's death. My friend Christine said I was going to get through it, but I wasn't sure if she was right.

I called Christine up again a couple of days later, wanting to talk to someone who'd been through what I was going through. "Does your body still hurt?" she asked. I told her it did. The pain from crying hadn't gone away.

Adam and the boys came home later that day, and I hugged them all so hard. I appreciated them so much, and I felt even more lucky to have them in my life. I also decided to take some of Christine's advice, and resume activities that made me feel like me. I got on the stationary bike in our basement and took myself through a spin class. I lifted weights. And that Wednesday, I went to my hockey scrimmage. It had been three weeks since I last played, and I needed to get back on the ice. I needed to feel that rush.

I walked into the dressing room, and while I looked like a pale, sad shell of myself, there was a smile on my face because I knew I was back to play this game I'd fallen in love with. Nobody there knew that my mum had passed away, and I kept it that way.

"Evanka!" my pal MJ said as soon as I walked in, which made me smile even bigger. "Great to see you!" she added as she moved over on the bench to make room for me. "I was away last week, but I'm back," I told her from behind a mask.

When I got on the ice, I was grinning ear to ear for the first time in a long time. Visiting Lara made me feel more like myself, and this was yet another step in that direction. Coach Ethan tapped my shin pads with his stick and said, "Welcome back!" Then we started our warm-up skate, and went right into the scrimmage. This game had long been my escape from worrying about my mum, and that day it was distracting me again in the way I needed.

Our scrimmage was the usual, with no coaches on the bench, no referees on the ice. It was just Coach Ethan out there. From time to time, he'd blow his whistle if he wanted to give us a quick in-game lesson. I was near the end of a shift, and had the puck in the corner in our offensive zone. Betty, a defender on the other team, was all over me, trying to get the puck off me. I was shielding that puck with my body, and I was trying to look up to see if a teammate was open somewhere, to see where I should send the puck next. I was holding on to it, keeping it close to my stick, moving side to side.

I looked up and saw my teammate Lisa behind the net, and I rimmed the puck around the boards to her, and she went for the wraparound—what a play, Lisa! The goalie, Teresa, made the save. Then Ethan blew his whistle, and he started skating toward me.

Uh-oh, I thought. *Did I do something wrong? Here comes a lesson. Yikes.*

"Notice how Evanka didn't throw the puck away?" Coach yelled, gesturing at me with his stick. "She keeps it with her until she has an open pass, or a moment to break free." Then he smacked his stick against the ice a few times, and so did my teammates. "Great play!" Ethan said, giving me a tap on the shin pads again.

Did I just get recognized for something good?

It felt like I'd won an Oscar: Best at Shielding the Puck and Making a Great Pass Under Pressure goes to . . . Evanka Osmak!

I was blushing behind my cage. Had I ever been prouder on the ice? I don't think so. This was the very first time Coach had called me out for something on the ice. And don't get me wrong, because there were plenty of times Ethan could have blown his whistle and said, "See how Evanka keeps falling on her butt? Don't do that!" But he'd never called me out for falling. (Thank you, Coach.) Instead, I got a compliment.

I skated back to the bench, trying not to smile too hard, like an eight-year-old kid who'd been told she's the best on the team.

"Awesome work!" MJ said as I got to the bench, smacking me on the pants. I hadn't smiled like that in weeks. And my goodness, had I ever needed that. As I left the dressing room that morning, I looked back and waved at my teammates, calling, "See you next week!"

The power of sport to create a community of women supporting each other is truly incredible, isn't it?

Slap Shot

Gosh, what a breath of fresh air.

That's what I said to Adam about my new co-anchor a week into our time together on the desk. Yes, I compared Ken to an actual breath of fresh air. Because he honestly was.

Ken was super fun. He started counting how many times we heard "Pucks in deep" during interviews. "Pucks in deep," as I quickly discovered, is one of his favourite phrases, and it's something a lot of hockey players say during in-game interviews.

For example, a reporter might ask: "How will you turn this game around?"

The player might respond with: "You know, we've just gotta get pucks in deep and keep putting pressure on them and getting our chances."

Counting those references absolutely thrilled Ken, and I found it hilarious and odd that this was one of his first ideas when we started working together. It told me this guy was instantly comfortable here, comfortable enough to be counting "pucks in deep" references, and smiling every time he heard one. The moment I met him, he started telling me darn near everything about himself. How he grew up in

Pictou, Nova Scotia (where?). About his insane collection of hockey cards. About how his high school gym teacher would kick kids out of class for taking "moon ball" shots from way out there. "Do you believe that?" he asked. About how much he loved music. Ken was funny, laid-back, comfortable in his skin. This much was clear to me after our first couple of conversations.

"They hired me to make you sound smarter," he told me, grinning. "I can really help you out there, Osmak." This guy was already calling me by my last name. Okay, then.

By day three, Ken was dropping lines from what I discovered was one of his favourite movies, *Slap Shot*. Anytime the Florida Panthers were mentioned on the air, he'd quip: "I was in Florida once on a southern tour," and look over at me for a reaction.

"The jukebox ate my quarter!" he'd tell me, eyebrows up, again looking for my reaction.

"Don't you remember *Slap Shot*?" he asked me.

"I haven't seen it," I said.

You should have seen the look on Ken's face: Incredulous. Jaw nearly on the floor. Eyes as wide as can be. Barely-there eyebrows as high as they could possibly go.

"Whaaaaaaaat!" he said. "HOW IS THAT EVEN POSSIBLE, OSMAK? You can't be serious."

Of course, I'd heard of *Slap Shot*. And being a sports fan, I'd seen clips of the movie before, for sure. It's about a tiny American town's crappy minor league hockey team, the Charlestown Chiefs, who were in their final season and had a cast of real characters, like the Hanson brothers, who loved to drop the gloves (fight). The movie is famous, but I'd never had the urge to sit down and watch the whole thing. Honestly, I'm not much of a movie watcher.

To Ken, this was a sign that he had to teach me important life lessons. And this became the running joke from about the moment we met, that I'm incredibly sheltered. He'd teach me slang words. Music. About pop culture. "Where did you grow up?" he'd ask. "Did your parents let you out of the house?"

Worldly Ken from Pictou, trying to teach me about life.

And what became immediately clear to me was that Ken didn't take this job overly seriously, and I mean that in the best way. He cared about his job, he had an incredible knowledge of sports (he's a total hockey nerd), but he approached the role in a laid-back way. He was the first on-air talent from whom I'd seen that. And about a week into our working together, he turned to me and said the most important thing anyone in sports media has ever said to me: "Hey, just be yourself on the desk."

It seems so obvious, but it was honestly such an eye-opening moment. It stemmed in part from the conversations he and I would have away from the desk when we were getting to know each other.

"These conversations we're having in the newsroom, let's do that on the desk," he told me. "Let's talk like friends chatting about sports. Let's bring this same energy."

Ever since I started in broadcasting, I was trying to be someone else, or a perfect version of an anchorwoman, afraid of making a mistake and feeling backlash. Thank goodness social media didn't exist in my early years of broadcasting, because I would have been roasted. And I would have taken the criticism incredibly hard. Seeing the online comments now was more than enough for me.

It wasn't long after Ken started that Sportsnet added Friday prime-time shows to our roster. It meant Ken and I spent more time together on weekends than we did with our family and friends. Our last show of the weekend was at one o'clock on Monday morning. It was busy, and there were also long breaks between games, which is how Ken and I got to know each other so fast. He told me more than once that he was the hockey-obsessed kid in his small town, that his grade five teacher even wrote in his yearbook: "You'll get to see the Canadiens at the Forum one day." Which he did, with his dad and his brother, Peter. Ken has this energy, this zest, this genuine love for sport, and we shared that. We'd tell endless stories, talk for hours. Between shows, we'd go for walks. We'd go see a movie (never *Slap Shot*, though). We'd have dinner. It was instant bonding. It was like having a second big brother.

Ken would make fun of himself nonstop on set. And it's not that this wasn't my personality before, because I love a good joke about myself—check out my boat-sized feet!—but Ken is the one who really showed me that if you can't laugh at yourself, what fun can you really have? That was big in terms of bringing me out of my shell.

"Make fun of me more," he told me. "I don't care—do it! It'll be great."

A couple months into working with Ken, I started to feel less like a robot. It had only taken four years to get there. Even my mum told me she'd noticed a change. "You guys look like you're having fun," she told me one morning over the phone. "I can see a difference. Ken should come for dinner one night!"

Ken would never say no to a free meal. He came out to Oakville to meet Borden and Jeannie, and I kid you not, after that dinner, my parents invited Ken and his wife to their annual Christmas party. Over the years they got to know Ken better and better, and they loved that he had the same energy and storytelling ability in person that they saw on TV.

When Martine went on maternity leave in 2012, Ken and I moved from weekends to weeknight shows. Prime time, sports fans! By then, he'd been there nearly six months (a record for my co-anchor!). Finally, I felt like I had consistency when it came to who I was sitting beside on the desk, and it meant we had a rhythm and knew each other well. It helped our dynamic on camera.

Ken wasn't the only consistency in my life, either. Adam and I had decided that we, us, were it. He proposed one Friday night in November of 2011: I got home from work around midnight, and our condo was decorated with pictures and mementos from trips and dates we'd been on. On the wall was a sign that read: "Will you marry me?" My jaw dropped and I jumped into Adam's arms. I yelled, "Yes!" and he slid a beautiful ring on my finger. He'd even asked my dad for permission.

I was so happy in my personal life, and I was the happiest I'd been at work, too. I was finally comfortable on the desk, on camera. I was having fun, the closest I'd been to truly being myself at work.

I took another big step toward feeling like myself at Sportsnet a couple of years later, in August of 2013, when a talent coach from Texas came into the studio. If Ken was the first person to cue a change in my behaviour on air, this talent coach, Doug, was the second. I had been on TV for six years, but this was the first time I'd gotten to work with someone whose job was to try to make me better. Doug had worked with talent at ESPN and Fox and other major networks. He'd watched tapes of Ken and me, and shared his thoughts, sitting down with us both individually.

"I really like what I see," he told me, which took me by surprise. And then Doug gave the best tip I've ever received when it comes to addressing a camera: "When you're writing your on-camera scripts, make it sound as though you're talking to someone on the phone—someone who understands sports, but doesn't know the intricacies," he said. "How would you talk to that person?"

Doug left me with that advice, and when he came back, he said he'd seen an improvement in me. "And I really like what you and Ken are doing together—there's a chemistry there," Doug said. "It truly comes across that it's two good friends talking sports. The comfort you have with one another is really obvious."

That's when I started to recognize that what Ken and I had was unique and kind of awesome. It made sense, too, because we weren't just co-workers, we were in each other's lives. We spent time together and had stories to tell. We were great friends. He was a guest at my wedding.

Adam and I had even travelled to Kenny's hometown in 2015 for the annual Lobster Carnival. I met Ken's mom for the first time, and his aunt and uncle. Adam and I stayed over at their place, and it was an absolute riot. It was so nice to see the hometown he referenced all the time; I could put pictures to so many of his stories.

And obviously it isn't always rosy between Ken and me—we fight and argue, too. Maybe three times a year, and usually around the NHL playoffs, when we're working a lot and we're around each other too much. There's a classic ebb and flow to our fights, where he'll say something he thinks is funny, and I'll find it inappropriate. I'll shut down, stop talking to him, other than on air. Maybe a day later, I'll tell him I think what he said was dumb, and he'll apologize, even if I'm being overly sensitive.

Ken is my biggest cheerleader and supporter, and none of our fights last long. We feel a bit like family, because we pick on each other constantly and know each other so well, but there's also a heavy dose of mutual respect there.

Years later, Ken and I would travel all over Canada for Hockey Day in Canada coverage. To Corner Brook, Yellowknife, Swift Current, and Victoria. And he's the one who encouraged me to be out on the ice playing hockey years later for the celebrity Hockey Day in Canada game, just a year after I'd started playing.

"Nobody will care if you aren't a star out there," Ken told me. "Quit taking yourself so seriously and just have fun!"

Not long after that game in Owen Sound in January of 2023, a viewer sent me a flash drive of the movie *Slap Shot*, after Ken quoted the movie on set for the millionth time, then said, "Osmak hasn't even seen it. Do you believe that?"

I do appreciate the gesture from the viewer who sent me the movie, but I'm never, ever plugging that flash drive in. I want to continue Ken's deep concern that I've never seen *Slap Shot*.

And from the number of clips Ken has already shown me, honest to God, I basically know the whole plot, word for word.

She Shoots, She Scores!

*O*h *my goodness. No way.*

   It went in!

I'd been waiting for this moment, to feel this feeling, for six whole months. And it finally happened: I just scored my first goal in a scrimmage. It felt like I'd just finished a marathon and achieved a personal best. Or won the spelling bee. Or climbed a massive mountain people said I couldn't climb. It felt unreal!

MJ had me wrapped in a hug, but I didn't think any of my other teammates knew how big this moment was for me. MJ definitely did. She's scored plenty of times and had been telling me in the last couple of weeks: "It's coming, Evanka!"

And here it was! The game wasn't even halfway over, but I wanted to rush off the ice and call Adam. He needed to know I put one in the net! And what would George say when I told him? Probably something like: "Finally, Mom."

But oh, what a feeling. This feeling was the best.

I can't tell you how my first goal went in with any degree of detail. It was such a blur. I think I picked up the puck on a rebound and shoveled it past the goalie. Something like that. There was no celebration, or celly, as the kids say. I didn't yell, "That's my first goal!" But I was absolutely beaming. Coach Ethan skated over to the bench after and held out his glove and I high-fived it. "Good work," he said, grinning. You better believe Coach knew how big this was for me. "Once you get the first one out of the way, the rest keep coming," Coach said. "It's like opening a floodgate. You'll be a thirty-goal scorer this season for sure."

"Thanks, Coach!" I said.

He might've been stretching the truth there, but still, you couldn't wipe the smile off my face. And yet I'd never wanted a scrimmage to end faster. Once it was over, I beelined off the ice and ran to the dressing room and got my stuff off as fast as I could. I ran out to the car and dialled Adam even before the keys were in the ignition.

"Guess what?" I said when he picked up, skipping a greeting altogether. "I SCORED!"

The noise Adam made after—cheering, at the top of his lungs—was so loud I had to turn down the volume in the car. "I'm so proud of you!" he said, still yelling. "Look out, Poulin!" The great No. 29, Marie-Philip Poulin, of course, has scored more than a few game-winners for Canada. Adam asked for the play-by-play, then asked me to please wait until the whole family was home to tell George and Blake, because he wanted to see their reactions to Mom's big moment.

Once I hung up with Adam, I called Ken. Yes, Kenny was the second person I told, because he's been incredibly supportive of my hockey journey. I knew he'd be just as happy for me, and he'd demand to know exactly how it crossed the line. And, of course, he did.

"I battled in front of the net and put it in!" I told him.

Ken was cheering like his Montreal Canadiens had just won a big game. "Way to get in the dirty areas, Osmak!" he said.

I didn't save the actual puck, but just before I headed into work that night, I grabbed one from my hockey bag, and of course I showed it off and presented it as *the* goal puck. Ken gave me a hearty high five, let out a big "Woo!" and then grabbed the puck and put tape on the side so he could write on it, like the pros do for big milestones. Like they do for rookies who pot their first in the NHL, like they did for Sidney Crosby's incredible 120-point season back in 2006–7.

Ken wrote: "FIRST GOAL!" in black Sharpie on the side of that puck, and I knew what was coming when we got on the air. During our second-period intermission update with Caroline Cameron and the Hockey Panel, Ken brought up my goal and I showed off the (pretend) puck. They all cheered, and I beamed for the second time that day.

It really took me back to being a kid. These games don't mean anything, and we switch up teams every week, but scoring made me so happy. And I imagine every time Georgie scores, he's feeling the exact same way. It's a feeling that I hope everyone gets to experience in some way.

I wish I could have called my mum to let her know. She's been gone nearly a year now, and if she were here, she would've been my second call, after Adam. She would've been so proud of me. It was Jeannie, after all, who'd encouraged me to start playing field hockey, the first team sport I fell in love with.

It wasn't until the next morning that I told George and Blake, while Adam was still home. It was a family moment. "Boys," I told them, holding up the puck, my big milestone puck. "I scored!"

Blake cheered and high-fived me. George's jaw dropped, and he ran in a circle in the living room, jumping up and down. "Way to go, Mom!" he said, wrapping me in the biggest hug he could muster. "It feels pretty good, doesn't it?"

It sure does, Georgie. It absolutely does.

Closure

The moment I set foot in our home on March 6, 2023, after all the renovations were completed, my eyes welled up with tears. I felt so many emotions. I was so happy. Excited. Relieved. And I was thinking of my mum.

I hadn't been by the house in a couple of weeks, so I hadn't seen the finishing touches yet. It wasn't until I walked through the main floor and got to the kitchen that the tears really started to fall. "She would've loved this," I told Adam, because Jeannie truly would have. Our kitchen was just like hers.

My mum had been gone just over a year, but so much about our home reminded me of her. The many design decisions she helped with and influenced, and even the ones she didn't have a say in because she couldn't speak anymore and didn't seem to have an interest. I wished so much that she was here to see the finished product: The red brick outside, the dark walnut floors, the layout of the main-floor bathroom. Jeannie influenced all of it.

When she still had a voice and enthusiasm for design, Mum suggested that Blake's and George's rooms be connected by a bathroom they could share, but the architect working on our house tried to talk us out of it. "No, Evanks, you'll regret it if you don't do that," my mum told me. "Trust me on this one." I did trust her, and I'm so glad I did: It was clear after just two days living here. Do you have any idea what two little boys can do to a bathroom? Toothpaste and pee everywhere. Just picture the inside of the grossest bar bathroom you've ever seen, with pee everywhere but in the toilet. Like the Dance Cave in Toronto. That's basically their bathroom, plus gobs of toothpaste. I'm glad they share it and Adam and I don't have to wipe down our bathroom every time we're in it.

Of course, I want to call Jeannie and tell her she was so right, but I can't. I still pick up the phone to call her all the time and then realize she's not going to answer. This was especially tough on the first birthday without her, January 23, 2023, and the anniversary of her death, two days later. But since those are both so personal, and a lot of people rightfully wouldn't remember those dates, they aren't the toughest that I've found without Jeannie. Mother's Day takes the cake there. It's universally celebrated, it seems, and it's inescapable. You see so many mentions of moms every May. I didn't want to do anything to acknowledge it the year Jeannie died, but that was nearly impossible because even strangers who saw me with the kids wished me a happy one. Adam picked up on my cues and didn't mention it—he was so kind and sensitive about it, but it was still in my face, that constant reminder. I cried so many times on Mother's Day. I think it'll always be a tough day for me going forward.

The boys' birthdays are also hard. George turned five a couple of months after Jeannie died, and I teared up just thinking about how Nama would've loved to be there with balloons and cake and way too many presents. She would've loved to run around with Blake and Georgie the birthday boy. We had a party in the backyard with family and some of George's closest buddies. It was fun, but I missed my mum. I don't think that'll ever go away.

But as time passes, I realize the reminders of her aren't all sad, that so many of them make me smile. I cried less on my second Mother's Day without my mum than I did on the first without her. I still look at her photo every day, and while that used to make me sad, now it makes me smile. Adam and I took our time getting our furniture set up where we wanted it in our place after the renovations, and really thought about where we'd hang art and pictures so it would truly feel like home.

One of the first pictures I hung up, right near the door, is the last family picture the Osmak crew took together. It was just after my parents celebrated their fiftieth anniversary, in August of 2021. Jeannie hadn't yet been diagnosed with ALS, but all the signs that something was really wrong were there. My parents had a small family gathering at a golf course, and my mum wasn't her jovial self. She barely laughed or smiled, and wasn't all that social with the many friends who'd turned up to celebrate her and Tato. She'd started having a harder time walking by then, too.

Since we were all together that day, we arranged for a family photo shoot at my parents' house. There are a few of us all together, and in one, we're all standing in the backyard—Nick, Amy, Kay, Chris, Adam, and I, and my parents are right in the middle, with their five grandkids standing in front. We're all grinning ear to ear. I printed that big family photo and framed it, and it's the first photo you see when you walk into our house.

Jeannie isn't here physically, but I still feel her presence everywhere. There's something incredibly special about that, and it took me a while to recognize. As time goes on, I realize my grief has changed. I can go into a rabbit hole of sadness and remember everything she's missing out on—it's too easy to get there, but I have less desire to go, since she's been gone four years now. It's exhausting to go there, and I've been there too many times. I'll think of her often, when I'm around the boys especially, since she loved them so much, and it's hard to not feel the immense grief that she's no longer with us. Instead, I try to think about all the wonderful things going on in my life and how happy Jeannie would be about them, which feels almost like a way forward. It's also beneficial to everyone around me. I'm trying, I really am.

That text my mum sent to Nick, Kay, and me a couple of days before she died, telling us how much she loves us? I've never been able to read it since that day. I can't. I think it'll shatter me all over again, and I don't want to put myself through that. I don't worry that she didn't know whether I loved her; she knew I did. But I wanted to be there to say goodbye, and I didn't make it to the hospital in time. That still eats at me to this day. I don't know if it ever won't. I keep reminding myself that the last time she saw me, the very last thing I said to her was "I love you." It doesn't get better than that.

These days, I still think of Jeannie every time I'm in our kitchen at home. There's a big island, the stove is to the right of the kitchen sink, the dishwasher is to the left. The floors are light brown hardwood, and the ceilings are nine feet, because Jeannie swore ten-footers were too tough to clean. It's the room in our house visitors always say they love, and it has a bunch of windows that look out on the backyard, giving it lots of natural light. Jeannie swore by the sink-under-the-window design.

I can't tell you how many times Adam has pointed out, "This kitchen really resembles your parents'."

"Do you think that's by accident?" I ask him.

She may be gone, but I still see Jeannie and her influence in so many ways, and it's a beautiful thing.

In the Groove

All right. I think I'm actually a threat on the ice. Really! It's a huge development in my hockey career, because I've noticed people are starting to play a little more aggressively with me. That means they see me as a threat, right?

It's January of 2024. I think people notice that I can keep up, and they're treating me like every other player out there instead of just waiting for me to fall and taking the puck like I've given it to them, gift-wrapped. I've come a long way since I first started scrimmaging more than two years ago. Last season, I'd get the puck and pass it to a better player, but then I started to realize I wasn't going to get any better if I didn't try to carry the puck a little more. So I started to, and as I handled the puck more, I developed a little bit more skill and, dare I say, confidence. It felt good.

"Ken, I had my first welcome-to-the-Bigs moment," I tell him. "I got a few elbows, a couple nudges, from some of the women in the game today. I think I'm being targeted."

"Way to go, Osmak!" he says. "I hope you elbowed them back."

I didn't, because that's not my game. Listen, I'm tall and maybe I could use my frame to my advantage, but it has never crossed my mind to be aggressive. I'm still finding my comfort zone out there. Plus, I don't want to piss anyone off because we're there to have fun. I'm more cautious in my older years than when I was tearing up the field hockey pitch. I don't want to leave in an ambulance, I don't wany anyone else to leave in an ambulance or get stretchered off the ice. I'm happy to be on a team and get a good workout in. That's the objective.

A couple games ago, one woman hacked at me and my stick dropped to the ice and I actually said: "Dude, what's your problem? You're always doing that." Because she is. She's overly aggressive. That's too chippy for me, so I called her out, because it's almost dangerous. MJ has also talked to her and told her to tone it down.

Once she got to the bench, she leaned over to me and said: "I'm really sorry, that was my fault." I accepted her apology and moved on. I decided I'll have a short memory, because I'm too busy trying to score! While I'm not quite the thirty-goal scorer Coach Ethan told me I'd be, I have gone on a few streaks, thank you very much. To me, a streak qualifies as three or more games in a row with a goal, and I've managed that three times so far!

I'm really proud of it, but I do get super humbled as soon as I tell my kids, who always expect me to score not one, but two or more goals per game. Sorry, kids, your mom doesn't have quite the skill of Natalie Spooner or Connor McDavid.

Blake is the only member of my family who's actually seen me play hockey, live and in person, because Wednesday-morning games are tough to make for a kid in school and a husband who works. Blake is nearly three years old now, and he's come to a few of my games and watched from the stands. That feeling I used to get when my parents would show up in the stands to one of my high school games is the same as having Blakey Baby there to see me. Having someone there who you care so much about is great. And he's really good at cheering and clapping randomly, in between chomping on snacks.

One night recently at work, I was asked about my latest goal streak. "I'm up to four!" I tell Caroline Cameron and the Hockey Panel. They're very invested in my career, and it comes up a lot. It's silly and fun, and I play right into it. "I scored off the rebound today," I tell them. "I stuck with it, went after that puck and fought off a defender and hammered it home."

"Osmak always scores from the dirty areas," Ken says.

"I try to score from any area," I say. "I'll take what I can get."

Then I make fun of Ken for being an overzealous hockey dad to his son, who's a goalie, and tell him he'd probably be super upset if he let in a soft goal or two. "You're a little obsessed," I tell him. Before our show starts, Ken watches the online feed of his son playing. No joke, he doesn't miss a second: He's a serious hockey dad. And he continues to remind me that I'm going to be the same once my boys start playing competitively.

I've been at Sportsnet for nearly sixteen years now, and only four of them without Ken. I can't imagine working alongside anyone else at this point. We've been through everything together: marriage, kids, my mum dying, his sons growing up, my sons growing up, awesome trips together through work and outside of work, him writing books, and even me writing books now. It's rare because not many people have friends this close that they work alongside so often.

On a Tuesday night, Ken and I might do four shows, all after NHL games. Penguins-Capitals at nine thirty, after the Oilers game at ten thirty, after the Canucks game at midnight, and after the Leafs game if they're on the West Coast, at one a.m. It's a lot of time together. We have so much fun, but also I'm often thinking, "Oh my God, I could murder this guy!" So many times a night.

Honestly, he's great at what he does, and his ideas are good ones. It's just that working so much with one person, you naturally wear on each other. We always come to an understanding. We never fight long because we're good friends and it's never worth it. We also know that our relationship is unique. I'm completely myself and so is he. We're vulnerable, and yet we work together and there's a professionalism there. Ken is legitimately the best teammate I could ever have.

And that's one of the reasons I'm the happiest I've ever been at work. Things at Sportsnet have changed so much since I started there in 2007, when there were eight or nine anchors across the country. Now we have six, and I consider myself and Ken lucky to be two of them.

I'm also the happiest in my personal life. I feel like I've won the lottery of life with my little family I co-created. The kids are at such fun ages. George is well-rounded and up for any sport, Blake is crushing soccer, and they can both have long conversations about just about anything. Both boys are curious and innocent. Always asking questions or showing off their latest talents and tricks. As exhausting and tiring as parenting can be, they're continuously sparking my inner child.

The other big factor that explains why I'm so happy these days is my girlfriends. We're making an effort to see one another more, to do more together, to have fun together. And it's the best.

A few years ago, I felt like I was stuck in a boring rut, consumed by work, family, and day-to-day chores. There was no spontane-ity. I've come to acknowledge that this can happen in your thirties, when we don't prioritize ourselves. That definitely happened to me around the time I started having kids.

Looking back, I know that's also what I appreciate about taking up and playing hockey in my forties. When I get in that dressing room, people might talk about their kids for a minute or two, and then it's all about hockey and our skill development and a new show MJ's watching and whatever the heck we feel like discussing that day. And that's part of what I'd been missing, I've realized. Something just for me.

Maybe it's an age thing, or re-prioritizing friendships. I'm not certain, but I know it's a positive shift, because I'm having more fun now with people who share my priorities. I thrive off my friend-ships, especially with girlfriends, and I think being isolated dur-ing the COVID pandemic really highlighted that, because I really needed those friendships to feel like myself.

My girlfriends have not only been there for fun times, but they've gotten me through and continue to help me through the hardest times. I don't know what I would've done to cope with my mum's passing if I didn't have my friends to lean on. Cultivating those friendships has been so rewarding. It's been everything, and with new friends and old.

Despite the terrible loss I've endured and all the ways I've found to cope with it, I find myself as happy as I've ever been in my for-ties. In my twenties, I was having a lot of fun, but also trying to navigate my career and really sort out what I wanted to do for a living, and where. In my thirties I was trying to find a partner, have kids, build a family. In my forties? I'm just enjoying everything I've worked for. I imagine my fifties will only get better. At least, that's what I hope for.

Most of all, I've settled into myself, into my age, into me. I'm confident, and I know myself better. I'm not nervous about what other people think about me because I've been in my own damn skin for forty-three years. This is it. This is me.

Out on the ice, I probably won't ever be the best at skating backward, and stopping on the right side is taking longer than I figured it would. Blake is four years old now and I'm teaching him to skate, and he's just as good at stopping as I am. We're both working on it.

Thankful

In January of 2023, I was standing in front of the net in the Harry Lumley Bayshore Community Centre in Owen Sound, Ontario, knees and hands shaking, mind racing. More than three thousand fans were watching me play hockey in person, and hundreds of thousands more were tuned into the Hockey Day in Canada Alumni game on TV.

I stood in front of that net, stick on the ice, and I watched NHL All-Star Wendel Clark pass me a puck that he'd told me would be coming my way if I planted myself in front of the net. I had done exactly that, obviously. When the former captain of the Toronto Maple Leafs gives you on-ice advice, you take it.

That pass hit my tape thanks entirely to Wendel's expert aim, and I managed to stay on my feet as I drew my stick back and slapped a wobbly and soft shot . . . just wide of the net. As I watched that puck go wide, I immediately turned and skated off the ice to take a seat on the bench. *I got a shot!* Too bad there was no rebound.

It's now a year later, and I've suited up again in the Hockey Day in Canada Alumni game, this time in beautiful Victoria, BC. I don't have the thoughts I had the previous year, about how in the world I got here, as I take the ice alongside former NHLers and Olympic gold medallists. But I'm still intimidated. I wasn't sure I was going to play in the 2024 Alumni game.

"I don't know," I'd told Ken as I was considering it. "I'm still not very good, and the 'first time' thing is over, and now it feels like, 'Oh, you want another parade?' I have to lug all my stuff to Victoria, and there are so many local players in the game who want their time to shine, and they want to play with Wendel and Olympic champions like Jennifer Botterill and be coached by Lanny McDonald, and then here I am and I can't even take a pass, and I don't want to take away from their ice time, and some guys out there just want to prove themselves, and . . ."

"Osmak, cut it out—just play!" Ken told me. "It'll be fun, and we'll be on the same team. Even if you decide to just take one shift, you should play!" What a classic Ken Reid answer.

So I decided I would play, and once again I was on Wendel's team. He had the same advice for me this time around: "Just stay by the net, stay by the net." But as the game gets close, I'm staying on the bench, telling anyone and everyone to take a shift instead of me. I'm embarrassed about my lack of skill compared to theirs, and I'm shy. There are a lot of skilled players out there who care about the outcome. I take maybe four or five shifts all game, and once it's tied up in the third, there's no way I'm playing another shift this game. Ken and Lanny are pumping me up and telling me I'm doing great. I'd rather sit and watch.

It ends 7–5 for the other team, but someone decides we should do shootouts for fun. Our team's coach, Geoff Courtnall—a former NHLer who was born and raised here in Victoria—taps me on the shoulder. "You're up second, Osmak," he tells me. "You're our second shooter."

Oh no. "No, thank you," I tell Coach Courtnall.

"Come on, you've gotta go!" he insists with a smile. "You're in."

I can tell there will be no weaseling out of this. Ken is on my team, and he scored earlier in the game, which is very annoying because I'll never hear the end of that. The guy will gloat for weeks, maybe months. But he's been comforting me all day, being super encouraging, telling me I don't suck, and now it's no different. "You've got this, Osmak!" he says.

Wendel slides over toward me on the bench and gives me some advice. "You're a righty, so shoot on the right side, and aim for the corner," he tells me. I nod, like I've just been given the most important instructions of my life.

"Should I lift the puck?" I ask, which is a skill that I'm capable of maybe 40 per cent of the time (Wendel doesn't know that, though).

He shakes his head no. "Don't raise it," Wendel says.

Okay. I won't.

It's my turn to go, the second of five shooters for our team. All eyes are on me. The rink is maybe 75 per cent full, and there's a wave going around the bowl. I'm flustered and intimidated and very uncomfortable. I want to get this over as quickly as possible, but I can't skate fast enough.

I get to centre ice, and I skate as fast as I can toward the net while keeping enough composure to handle the puck. I cross over the blue line and take a few more strides, and then I take my stick back and look down and whack the puck along the ice on the right side and . . . boof! It hits the goalie's pad. No goal, but I hit the net. *Phew.*

I wish I could take another whack at the rebound, but I can't, because that's not a legal move in shootouts. You get one shot. As I circle around to skate back to the bench, I figure I should do something for the fans, because I'm a cheeseball, and I'm feeling relief that my shootout attempt is over, and I didn't fall and my shot actually hit the net.

So I throw an arm in the air and wave with my glove, just to get the people going, you know? I don't know if they even cheered, but that was my celebration. Was it a wave? A pump-up? A twitch in my arm? It's hard to tell. Thankfully, no one else on our team scored in the shootouts, except for Jennifer Botterill, who has three more Olympic gold medals than me, so that's fair.

After both teams shake hands, former NHLer-turned-broadcaster Kevin Bieksa looks at me and says, "You're not sweaty at all!"

"Yeah, I barely played," I tell him. I took the whole third period off, when the game was close. And while I had a good time at the 2024 Hockey Day in Canada Alumni game, I decide it'll be my last. I won't let Ken talk me into it again, no matter how hard he tries.

I know I'll continue playing hockey for as long as I can, because I love it. But I won't play on a big stage like that again. For someone who started at age forty-one to get to play with NHLers and Olympians, that's a once-in-a-lifetime chance that I got to do twice, and I'm happily calling it there.

This 2024 Hockey Day in Canada Alumni game reminded me that I don't need to take my game to the next level to feel fulfilled. My happiest place on ice is at my Wednesday-morning scrimmages with Skate Sister, and that's what makes me feel fulfilled and confident: It's enough. I'm not out there gunning to move up a level. I'm delighted that I've learned a new skill and made new friends and challenged myself. This truly has been a life-changing experience, and so much more than I could have asked for.

I was never here to become a star, but I proved to myself I could do this. Hockey has given me the confidence to know that I can try something new in the future, with less fear, and that I'll learn that new skill, and with the knowledge that learning something new is so much fun.

My personal hockey scouting report as of today is this: I'm a decent skater who's comfortable with crossovers right over left, but super shaky the other direction. I can stop on a near dime on the right, but the left still needs work. I can raise the puck if I'm trying to in practice about 40 per cent of the time, and I've raised it twice in games with my snap shot—both times were very exciting. I can score from close range. I'm not yet comfortable skating backward and I might never be. I feel most at home on the right wing, and I refuse to play defence. I'm comfortable going into the corners, digging for a puck and finding a teammate to hit with a pass. I've seen Auston Matthews do this countless times for the Toronto Maple Leafs, so it's in my brain; it's just a matter of executing. I tell myself: "What would Auston do?" And then I do it worse than he would.

That Skate Sister Cup sits in our arena, and I see it most weeks when I walk in the front doors. Quite honestly, I've never thought about winning it, because it has never been about winning for me. It's about me, and my enjoyment of hockey. It's not about my kids or my husband; I'm doing this for myself.

The exhilaration is there every week. I still step onto the ice before scrimmages and think, *Okay, don't fall.* I feel butterflies when the game starts and I'm on the ice, with the extra adrenaline pumping. I don't get that in any other day-to-day activity. Hockey has given me pride. Self-confidence. A bit of youthful vibrance. The feeling that I can try anything new.

When I challenged myself, it was simple: I wanted to learn how to play hockey, to have my rookie season at the age of forty-one, a tiny bit older than most when they pick this game up. And here I am, a hockey player, and the experience has given me so much more than I could have asked for.

I recently turned forty-five, and I'm starting to ask myself: *What's next?* Hockey has been a great experience, and I'll continue to play while I also look for another challenge. It doesn't have to be gruelling or expensive or time-consuming, but I don't ever want to stop learning.

I've always been active and motivated by physical health, and my focus now is on pursuing something to help keep my brain sharp. As I go through perimenopause and read up on research around what can happen to women—symptoms like brain fog and decreased memory and depression and anxiety—it makes me want to work harder to keep learning and expanding my mind.

I've started doing more Sudoku puzzles, and I'm reading the newspaper every day to stay informed. I've written a children's book about basketball called *Ali Hoops*, and I'm working on a second kids' book. I plan to start Ukrainian lessons soon, too. Jeannie spoke it well and Borden does, too. I want to be able to chat with him in Ukrainian, because the language and heritage are a big part of our family.

And family is among the reasons I have this curiosity, why I want to keep learning. It's something I've been thinking about more and more since I lost my mum: making good use of the time I have left. It's been a reawakening for me. I'm constantly asking: How am I improving myself?

I hope I never stop asking that question, and for that I have my mum to thank.

Acknowledgments

This book was a challenge in the most positive and wonderful way. It reminded me of some really happy memories from when I was a kid, transformative moments when I was chasing a crazy dream and then rediscovering that youthful joy into my forties. It was also a constant reminder that my mum was gone. It was hard to write.

I had the best partner with me the whole time. Thank you, Kristina, for listening, writing, deleting, elaborating, and constantly checking in. This absolutely doesn't get done without you.

Brian, thank you for taking a chance and asking if I would be interested in writing a book. And also for sticking with me and Kristina throughout this whole process.

Brittany, thank you for your unwavering support and advice. You not only helped shape this book; you confirmed our experience with your own personal journey.

My friends—I'm really fortunate that every chapter in my life has introduced me to some incredibly wonderful people. To those I met when I was in my single digits, to those who have been a big part of this next chapter called The Forties—thank you. I wish I could have listed all of them in this book, but I hope you know how special you all are.

I am so grateful to my family.

Adam—you are number one. You're the best at everything you do, which also involves being the best at handling me.

George and Blake—you constantly remind me how awesome it is to be your mom.

Tato, Katrusha, and Nicholas—I had so much fun reliving our family trips, visits, and happenings, and I only hope this book reminds you of how full a life we have had.

Mum—it still hurts that you're gone. I can still hear your words, remember your poise, and smile at your distinct, hearty laugh. I hope you'd enjoy this book as much as I did writing it.